THE POWER OF THE ORDINARY CITIZEN

How Everyday People Shape History, Economy, and Society

Abdellatif Raji

Yaraak Publishing House

is included for educational, commentary, and informational purposes, constituting "fair use" under applicable copyright laws. If you are the owner of copyrighted material referenced in this book and believe its use is not covered by fair use, please contact the publisher.

No Legal, Financial, or Professional Advice

The contents of this book do not constitute professional legal, financial, or political advice. The author and publisher recommend consulting with qualified professionals for guidance related to legal, financial, or political matters.

Non-Endorsement Clause

The mention of any person, organization, website, or company within this book does not imply an endorsement by the author or publisher. Likewise, any reference to third-party content, trademarks, or brand names is strictly for informational purposes and does not imply sponsorship, approval, or affiliation.

Reader Responsibility

The reader acknowledges that any actions taken based on the content of this book are done at their own discretion and risk. The author and publisher are not liable for the outcomes of personal decisions made in response to the information presented.

Updates & Revisions

The author and publisher reserve the right to update, modify, or revise the content of this book in future editions to reflect new insights, updated research, or changes in relevant policies.

ISBN (paperback): 978-1-963876-54-3
ISBN (hardcover): 978-1-963876-53-6
ISBN (digital): 978-1-963876-52-9

Printed in the United States of America

"To the ordinary citizens—past, present, and future—who dared to believe that their voices matter, their choices shape history, and their actions can change the world."

To the activists, the dreamers, the workers, the thinkers, and the fighters—this book is for you.

To the teachers who inspire, the workers who persevere, the voters who engage, and the voices that refuse to be silenced—your courage fuels progress.

To those who have ever felt powerless but chose to act anyway—may you find in these pages the proof that change is possible and that it begins with you.

And to everyone who refuses to accept the world as it is, knowing it can be better—you are the revolution.

This book is dedicated to you.

"The only thing necessary for the triumph of evil is for good men to do nothing."
— Edmund Burke

"Never doubt that a small group of thoughtful, committed citizens can change the world. Indeed, it's the only thing that ever has."
— Margaret Mead

"History is not made by those who wait."
— Barack Obama

These words serve as a reminder that passivity enables oppression, but action creates change. The power to shape the future has always belonged to those who dare to step forward.

ABDELLATIF RAJI

CONTENTS

FOREWORD

There has never been a more urgent time to recognize the power of the ordinary citizen. In a world dominated by corporate monopolies, political corruption, and a system designed to keep people complacent, it is easy to believe that one person cannot make a difference.
But that belief is a lie.

History has shown us time and time again that **change is never handed down from the top—it is demanded, fought for, and won by those at the bottom.** From the civil rights movements to labor strikes, from grassroots activism to digital revolutions, **it has always been ordinary people who have forced systems to bend, policies to change, and societies to evolve.**

This book is both a **wake-up call and a guide**. It is for anyone who has ever felt powerless in the face of injustice. It is for those who see problems in the world and wonder, **"What can I do?"** It is for every person who has been told that **their voice, their choices, and their actions don't matter.**

Through historical examples, real-world case studies, and **a practical roadmap for action**, *The Power of the Ordinary Citizen* will show you that:

- **You are more powerful than you think.**

- **Small, consistent actions lead to massive change.**

- The system is designed to make you feel powerless—because it fears you.

- If enough people act, governments, corporations, and elites must listen.

This is not a book about waiting for change. **It is a book about making change happen.**

The question is not whether the world can be different.
The question is: **Will you take part in shaping it?**

Let's begin.

PREFACE

There is a common myth that real power belongs only to politicians, billionaires, and corporations—that ordinary people are too small to make a difference. This myth is not just false; it is dangerous. It convinces people to stay silent, to comply, and to believe that the world is something that happens to them, rather than something they can shape.

This book was born out of a simple but powerful idea: **history is shaped by those who refuse to accept the status quo.** Every major movement, every shift in society, every hard-won right came not from the generosity of the powerful, but from **ordinary citizens who demanded change.**

As I wrote this book, I was inspired by the countless individuals —past and present—who chose action over apathy, courage over fear, and persistence over passivity. Whether it was **Rosa Parks refusing to give up her seat, Greta Thunberg striking for climate action, or anonymous workers organizing for better wages**, their stories all point to one truth:

You don't need to be famous, wealthy, or in a position of authority to make an impact. You just need to act.

This book is not just about inspiration; it is about **empowerment.** It provides historical context, real-world case studies, and **a step-by-step roadmap for reclaiming power in your daily life.** From where you spend your money to how you engage in politics, from the media you consume to the communities you build—**every choice you make either strengthens or weakens the systems that control society.**

This book is for:

- **Those who feel frustrated by the state of the world but don't know where to start.**
- **Those who want to challenge corrupt systems but feel like their voice doesn't matter.**
- **Those who are ready to take action, but need a strategy.**

If you have ever felt powerless, know this: **you are not.** The world is not run by the strongest or the wealthiest; it is shaped by the ones who **refuse to remain silent.**

The question is not **whether** you can make a difference—the question is: **Will you?**

Let's begin.

PROLOGUE

"There comes a time when silence is betrayal." — Martin Luther King Jr.

There is a quiet war happening every single day—a battle between apathy and action, between control and resistance, between those who hold power and those who are told they have none.

Most people don't even realize they are part of this war. They wake up, go to work, pay their bills, watch the news, and accept the world as it is. They feel frustrated about politics, inequality, corruption, and injustice, yet they convince themselves:

☐ *"I'm just one person. What can I really do?"*
☐ *"The system is too big. Nothing will ever change."*
☐ *"This is just how the world works."*

And this is exactly what those in power want you to believe. **Because the moment you stop believing in your own power, you hand it over to someone else.**

But what if I told you that the greatest shifts in history—the revolutions, the movements, the rights we enjoy today—were not started by the wealthy, the famous, or the powerful?

They were started by people just like you.

- A **young girl refused to give up her seat on a bus**, and the Civil Rights Movement gained momentum.

- A **high school student skipped school for climate action**, and millions followed.

- A **worker demanded fair wages**, and labor laws changed across the world.

These people were not superheroes. They had no special privileges. **They were ordinary citizens who simply decided that enough was enough.**

This book is not about abstract theories. It is not about waiting for politicians to save us. **It is about what you—one person—can do today to start making a difference.**

Because the truth is this:

☐ **The system survives because people do nothing.**
☐ **The world changes when enough people decide to act.**

This book will show you how.

You are not powerless. You never were.

The question is: **What will you do with the power you already have?**

Let's begin.

INTRODUCTION

"The world will not be destroyed by those who do evil, but by those who watch them without doing anything." — *Albert Einstein*

Look around. The world is full of problems: corrupt politicians, corporate greed, environmental destruction, rising inequality, and the erosion of basic freedoms. Every day, you hear about it on the news, see it on social media, and feel it in your own life. And yet, most people do nothing.

Not because they don't care.
Not because they don't see the problems.
But because they believe the **greatest lie ever told:**

 "I'm just one person. I have no real power."

This lie is the foundation of every oppressive system in history. The moment people believe they are powerless, they become easy to control. **Governments, corporations, and elites do not maintain power because they are stronger. They maintain power because people comply.**

This book exists to **shatter that illusion.**

Who This Book is For

This book is for:

✓ **The frustrated voter** who feels like the system is rigged.
✓ **The overwhelmed activist** who wants to make a difference but doesn't know where to start.
✓ **The everyday worker** struggling under unfair wages, corporate exploitation, and economic instability.
✓ **The concerned citizen** watching the world spiral out of control, wondering if their actions matter.

If you have ever felt **angry, helpless, or trapped**, this book is for you.

Because the truth is:

☐ **You are more powerful than you think.**
☐ **Small actions create massive ripples of change.**
☐ **History is shaped by those who refuse to remain silent.**

What You'll Learn

In these pages, you will discover:

☐ **How history proves that ordinary people—not elites—have always driven change.**
☐ **How corporations and governments manipulate you into believing you are powerless.**
☐ **How to reclaim control over your money, your politics, your media, and your community.**
☐ **How to take immediate action—without waiting for permission.**

This is not just a book—it is a **blueprint for action.** It will give you **real-world strategies** to start reclaiming your power today.

The Only Question Left: Will You Act?

You are at a crossroads. You can read this book, feel inspired, and then go back to business as usual. **Or you can decide—right now —that you will no longer be a passive observer of history.**

This is your moment.
 This is your call to action.
 What happens next is up to you.

Let's begin.

PART ONE: THE MYTH OF POWERLESSNESS

CHAPTER 1: THE ILLUSION OF INSIGNIFICANCE – WHY MOST PEOPLE BELIEVE THEY HAVE NO REAL IMPACT

From an early age, people are conditioned to believe that power lies in the hands of a select few—politicians, business tycoons, celebrities, and world leaders. The average person is often made to feel like just another cog in a massive machine, replaceable and unimportant. This belief is reinforced by media narratives, societal structures, and even the education system, which teaches compliance rather than empowerment.

This illusion of insignificance is no accident—it serves a purpose. When people believe their actions don't matter, they stop trying to change things. They don't vote because they think one ballot won't shift an election. They don't speak out because they assume no one will listen. They don't challenge injustice because they think someone else, someone "more powerful," should handle it.

But this belief is not only false—it is dangerous. It creates a passive society, one where citizens relinquish their influence and allow decisions to be made for them. Governments go unchecked, corporations exploit workers and consumers, and social injustices persist because too many people believe that their individual actions won't make a difference.

In reality, history has shown that every movement, every revolution, and every major shift in society began with ordinary people who rejected this illusion. The Civil Rights Movement in the U.S. didn't start in Washington; it started with everyday citizens demanding justice. The fall of oppressive regimes around the world didn't begin with leaders—it started when individuals, en masse, refused to comply.

The truth is simple: Every action, no matter how small, has the power to create ripples. Every purchase you make influences the economy. Every word you speak can inspire someone. Every decision you take contributes to the direction of society.

The illusion of insignificance is just that—an illusion. And once you recognize it for what it is, you take the first step toward reclaiming your power.

CHAPTER 2: DEFINING THE "ORDINARY CITIZEN" – WHO THEY ARE AND WHY THEY MATTER

The term "ordinary citizen" might sound like a description of someone unremarkable—just another face in the crowd. But in reality, the ordinary citizen is the most powerful force in any society. They are the workers, the parents, the students, the entrepreneurs, the voters, and the consumers. They are the people who make up the majority of any nation, yet they are often led to believe they have little influence over the course of history, politics, or the economy.

An ordinary citizen is not defined by wealth, status, or political connections. They are defined by their role in shaping society through their daily choices—what they buy, who they vote for, what values they uphold, and how they participate in their communities. Every great change in history has been fueled by individuals who started as "ordinary" but refused to remain silent.

Why They Matter

1. They Drive the Economy

- Every dollar spent is a vote for the kind of world people want to live in.

- Consumer choices influence what businesses succeed and which fail.

- Small businesses and local economies thrive because of everyday people supporting them.

2. They Shape Politics

- Elected officials only have power because citizens give it to them through voting.

- Grassroots movements led by regular people have changed laws and policies.

- Civic engagement, protests, and petitions all start with individuals who take action.

3. They Influence Culture

- Ordinary people dictate trends in fashion, music, and entertainment.

- Social movements, from civil rights to climate activism, started with everyday individuals challenging the norm.

- Social media has given regular people a louder voice than ever before.

The Silent Majority Must Become the Active Majority

The greatest weakness of the ordinary citizen is not a lack of power—it is a lack of belief in their own influence. When millions of people believe they are powerless, they hand over control to those who do believe in their power: politicians, corporations, and elites who have no incentive to prioritize the needs of the majority.

But when the ordinary citizen wakes up to their potential, they become unstoppable. They vote, they organize, they demand better policies, they hold the powerful accountable, and they change the direction of history.

Being an ordinary citizen is not a limitation—it is an opportunity. And the moment people recognize that, the world changes.

CHAPTER 3: HISTORICAL PROOF OF THE CITIZEN'S POWER – MOMENTS WHEN REGULAR PEOPLE CHANGED THE COURSE OF HISTORY

History is not shaped by kings, presidents, or billionaires alone—it is shaped by the collective action of ordinary citizens who refuse to accept injustice, oppression, or stagnation. Time and time again, everyday people have risen up, challenged the status quo, and forced monumental change. Below are some of the most powerful examples proving that ordinary citizens hold immense power when they take action.

1. The Civil Rights Movement (1950s–1960s, USA)

How Ordinary People Made a Difference:
The fight for racial equality in the U.S. was not won in the halls of Congress alone—it was driven by millions of ordinary citizens who boycotted, marched, and demanded justice.

Key Event: The Montgomery Bus Boycott (1955–1956)

- Sparked by Rosa Parks, an ordinary woman who refused to give up her seat to a white passenger, this movement led to the desegregation of public buses.
- Thousands of Black citizens boycotted the bus system for over a year, showing the power of economic resistance.
- This was a turning point that led to the Civil Rights Act of 1964.

Lesson:
One citizen's courage, amplified by collective action, can dismantle oppressive systems.

---

2. The Fall of the Berlin Wall (1989, Germany)

How Ordinary People Made a Difference:
For nearly three decades, the Berlin Wall symbolized division and oppression. However, it was not governments that tore it down—it was the sheer will of ordinary East and West Germans.

Key Event: The Peaceful Protests of Leipzig

- Throughout 1989, tens of thousands of East Germans began gathering for peaceful protests, demanding freedom.
- These protests grew, and security forces refused to fire on citizens, fearing mass backlash.
- Eventually, the pressure became too great, and the government collapsed—leading to the wall's fall and Germany's reunification.

Lesson:
A population united in peaceful resistance can bring down even the most oppressive regimes.

---

3. India's Independence from British Rule (1947)

How Ordinary People Made a Difference:
The British Empire, one of the most powerful colonial forces in history, was forced to withdraw from India—not because of war, but because of persistent, nonviolent resistance from millions of Indian citizens.

Key Event: The Salt March (1930)

- Led by Mahatma Gandhi, thousands of Indians marched 240 miles to the sea to produce their own salt, defying British salt laws.
- This symbolic act of resistance sparked nationwide civil disobedience, inspiring millions to protest against British rule.
- Over time, the movement led to the complete independence of India in 1947.

Lesson:
Economic and civil disobedience by ordinary citizens can dismantle even the most powerful empires.

---

4. The Arab Spring (2010–2012, Middle East & North Africa)

How Ordinary People Made a Difference:
The Arab Spring was a wave of uprisings against oppressive governments across the Middle East, sparked by a single act of protest by an ordinary citizen.

Key Event: The Self-Immolation of Mohamed Bouazizi (2010, Tunisia)

- Mohamed Bouazizi, a street vendor, set himself on fire in protest of government corruption and police brutality.

- His act triggered mass protests in Tunisia, which led to the overthrow of the government.
- This inspired uprisings across Egypt, Libya, Syria, and beyond, proving that one act of defiance can spark a revolution.

 Lesson:
One person's stand against oppression can ignite a movement that spreads across nations.

5. The Women's Suffrage Movement (Late 19th – Early 20th Century, Global)

 How Ordinary People Made a Difference:
For centuries, women were denied the right to vote. It was only through relentless activism by ordinary women that the world changed.

 Key Event: The Suffragette Hunger Strikes (UK & USA, Early 1900s)

- Women like Emmeline Pankhurst and Alice Paul led movements where women were imprisoned for demanding voting rights.
- Their hunger strikes and relentless activism forced governments to grant women the right to vote.
- Today, the right of women to vote is considered fundamental in most democracies worldwide.

 Lesson:
Persistence and unity in demanding rights can break down centuries-old oppression.

6. The Labor Movement & Workers' Rights (19th–20th Century, Global)

 How Ordinary People Made a Difference:
Before labor unions, workers were exploited with long hours, dangerous conditions, and no rights. It was ordinary factory

workers, miners, and laborers who organized strikes and protests to demand better conditions.

☐ *Key Event: The 8-Hour Workday Struggle*

- Workers across the U.S. and Europe fought for fair wages and humane working conditions.
- The 1886 Haymarket Affair in Chicago led to the recognition of the 8-hour workday.
- Over time, labor laws were changed, improving the lives of millions.

☐ *Lesson:*

When ordinary workers unite, they can force corporations and governments to respect their rights.

Final Thought: History is Written by Those Who Act

Each of these moments in history proves one thing: power is not confined to the wealthy, the politicians, or the elite. It belongs to **ordinary people** who recognize their collective strength and refuse to accept injustice.

The myth of powerlessness is the greatest lie ever told. Every significant movement that shaped our world began with regular people who decided they would not be ignored. **The question is not whether ordinary citizens have power—it is whether they will choose to use it.**

If history is proof of anything, it is this: when citizens rise, the world changes.

PART TWO: THE HIDDEN POWER OF THE ORDINARY CITIZEN

CHAPTER 4: THE ECONOMIC FORCE OF THE EVERYDAY CONSUMER

"Every dollar you spend is a vote for the kind of world you want to live in."

Many people believe that the economy is controlled solely by governments, multinational corporations, and financial institutions. While these entities have significant influence, the true economic power lies in the hands of the everyday consumer. The choices we make—where we shop, what we buy, and the businesses we support—shape industries, impact corporate policies, and even drive social and environmental change.

The idea that ordinary consumers have little influence is **a myth**. In reality, history has shown that when people collectively decide to demand better products, ethical business practices, and social responsibility, companies and industries are forced to adapt.

1. How Consumers Shape Markets and Industries

The Power of Demand

- Companies produce what people buy—if demand for a product increases, businesses scale production to meet it.
- When consumers shift preferences (e.g., moving from fast food to healthier options), entire industries transform.
- **Example:** The rise of plant-based diets has forced fast-food chains to introduce vegan menu items.

Consumer Spending as a Form of Voting

- Every purchase supports a business model. When people buy ethically sourced products, they encourage sustainable practices.
- Boycotts have proven to be one of the most effective tools in forcing corporate accountability.
- **Example:** The boycott against Nestlé in the 1970s (over unethical marketing of baby formula) led to global changes in business ethics.

Case Study: The Organic & Sustainable Product Movement

- In the 1990s, organic and eco-friendly products were niche markets.
- As consumer demand grew, major retailers (Walmart, Target, Amazon) were forced to stock sustainable products.
- Today, organic food and sustainable goods are billion-dollar industries.

2. How Ethical Consumerism Changes Business Practices

Boycotts That Changed Corporate Behavior

- **Nike Sweatshop Scandal (1990s):** After public pressure, Nike reformed its labor practices.
- **BP Oil Spill (2010):** A widespread consumer backlash forced BP to invest billions in environmental restoration.
- **H&M's Sustainability Efforts:** Following consumer criticism, H&M launched its Conscious Collection and recycling programs.

Fair Trade & Ethical Sourcing Movements

- Consumers demanding fair wages for workers in developing countries led to the **Fair Trade** certification.
- This forced brands like Starbucks, Ben & Jerry's, and Whole Foods to incorporate fair-trade ingredients.

The Rise of Second-Hand and Circular Economies

- The popularity of resale platforms like ThredUp, Poshmark, and Facebook Marketplace is reducing fast fashion waste.
- Minimalism and zero-waste lifestyles are reshaping product packaging and production.

---

3. The Power of Small Businesses and Local Economies

Why Supporting Local Businesses Matters

- For every **$100 spent at a local business, $68** stays in the community (compared to $43 at a national chain).
- Local businesses create jobs, strengthen communities, and reduce environmental impact.
- The "Buy Local" movement is growing as consumers seek higher quality and personalized services.

Examples of Consumer-Driven Small Business Success

- **The Rise of Farmer's Markets:** Consumer demand for

fresh, local food has led to thousands of farmer's markets worldwide.

- **Independent Bookstores vs. Amazon:** Communities rallying behind local bookstores have helped many survive the digital era.
- **Microbreweries & Artisanal Brands:** Small craft breweries and handmade goods have flourished due to consumer preference for quality over mass production.

4. Using Consumer Power for Social Change

The Link Between Consumer Behavior and Social Justice

- Supporting Black-owned, women-owned, and minority-owned businesses can help close economic disparities.
- Conscious shopping can promote sustainability, fair wages, and human rights.
- Apps and websites now allow consumers to check the ethics of brands before buying.

How to Use Your Buying Power Effectively

1. **Do Research:** Look into a company's labor policies, environmental impact, and supply chain.
2. **Support Ethical Brands:** Choose companies committed to sustainability and fair trade.
3. **Buy Local:** Strengthen small businesses and keep money within your community.
4. **Reduce & Reuse:** Participate in the circular economy to minimize waste.
5. **Use Social Media to Influence Change:** Call out unethical companies and support ethical ones.

Final Thought: You Have More Economic Power Than You

Think

Consumers are not powerless—they are the **lifeblood of the global economy**. The money we spend (or choose not to spend) has the potential to reshape industries, promote ethical business practices, and drive social change.

The world's biggest corporations **listen** to consumers because their survival depends on it. If enough people demand better products, fair wages, and responsible business practices, companies will be forced to comply.

The question is not whether you have economic power—the question is: **Are you using it wisely?**

CHAPTER 5: HOW DAILY PURCHASING DECISIONS SHAPE MARKETS AND INDUSTRIES

Every time you make a purchase—whether it's a cup of coffee, a smartphone, or a pair of sneakers—you are influencing the economy in ways you may not realize. Consumer choices dictate what products succeed, which industries thrive, and how companies operate. The power of individual and collective purchasing decisions has reshaped markets, forced companies to adopt new practices, and even driven social and environmental change.

1. Consumer Demand Drives Production

Businesses exist to serve consumer needs, and when those needs change, industries must adapt or risk failure.

- **If people buy more electric cars → Automakers shift focus to EV production.**

- **If consumers demand healthier food → Fast food**

chains introduce plant-based options.

- **If fashion trends favor sustainability → Brands are forced to use eco-friendly materials.**

Case Study: The Plant-Based Food Boom

- A decade ago, plant-based foods were a niche market.
- As more consumers sought healthier, ethical, and sustainable food choices, companies responded.
- Today, nearly every major fast-food chain offers plant-based options (McDonald's, Burger King, KFC).

2. Boycotts and Public Pressure Reshape Corporate Policies

When consumers withdraw their spending from unethical companies, businesses are forced to change.

Examples of Consumer-Led Business Transformations:

- **Nike (1990s):** After exposure of sweatshop labor, global boycotts forced Nike to improve working conditions.
- **Nestlé (1970s–Present):** Ethical concerns over baby formula marketing and deforestation led to policy changes.
- **BP Oil Spill (2010):** Massive backlash forced BP to invest billions in environmental restoration efforts.

Boycotts are proof that **money talks**—when companies face financial losses, they listen to consumers.

3. The Rise of Ethical Consumerism and Conscious Buying

More consumers today prioritize **ethical, sustainable, and socially responsible** businesses.

- **Fair Trade Products:** Coffee, chocolate, and clothing brands have adopted fair-trade practices due to consumer demand.

- **Sustainable Fashion:** The rise of second-hand clothing platforms (ThredUp, Poshmark) has forced fast fashion brands to rethink wasteful practices.
- **Cruelty-Free Beauty:** Companies like Lush and The Body Shop gained popularity by refusing to test on animals, influencing major brands to follow suit.

Case Study: The Fall of Single-Use Plastics

- In response to consumer demand, companies like Starbucks, McDonald's, and Coca-Cola have phased out plastic straws.
- Supermarkets are reducing plastic packaging, offering reusable options.
- Public awareness campaigns about ocean pollution have driven governments to ban single-use plastics.

---

4. Small Businesses and Local Economies Thrive on Consumer Choices

Supporting small businesses strengthens communities and shifts economic power away from corporate monopolies.

- **Buying Local = More Money Stays in the Community**
  - For every **$100 spent at a local business, $68** stays in the local economy (vs. $43 at big chains).
  - Local businesses hire locally, invest in communities, and foster innovation.
- **Success Stories of Consumer-Driven Small Business Growth:**
  - **The Growth of Farmers' Markets:** Consumer demand for fresh, locally sourced food has made farmers' markets a $9 billion industry.
  - **Independent Bookstores Surviving Amazon:** Community support has allowed local bookstores to compete with online giants.
  - **Craft Breweries vs. Corporate Beer:** The rise

of independent breweries shows consumers value quality over mass production.

5. The Future: Consumers as Industry Game-Changers

The next wave of industry transformation will be driven by consumer expectations.

- **Sustainable Energy:** As more people install solar panels and buy electric vehicles, the energy industry is shifting toward renewables.

- **Tech & Data Privacy:** Consumers demanding privacy-friendly alternatives are forcing tech giants to reconsider data policies.

- **Meat Alternatives:** Lab-grown and plant-based meats are rapidly growing due to ethical and environmental concerns.

Final Thought: Every Purchase is a Vote

Every time you spend money, you are shaping the world. Companies only succeed when people buy their products. If enough consumers prioritize ethics, sustainability, and innovation, businesses will have no choice but to follow.

The question is: **Are you using your purchasing power to create the world you want to live in?**

CHAPTER 6: THE RISE OF ETHICAL CONSUMERISM AND ITS IMPACT

In the past, consumers primarily focused on price, quality, and convenience when making purchasing decisions. But today, an increasing number of people are considering something more: ethics. Ethical consumerism—the practice of buying products and services that align with personal values, such as environmental sustainability, fair labor practices, and social responsibility—has become a powerful force in the global economy.

This shift in consumer mindset is not just a trend; it is **reshaping industries, forcing corporations to adopt responsible practices, and driving meaningful social and environmental change.**

1. What is Ethical Consumerism?

Ethical consumerism means making purchasing decisions based on moral values rather than just price or brand loyalty. Consumers today are increasingly asking:

✔ *Was this product made using child labor?*
✔ *Is this company harming the environment?*
✔ *Does this brand support human rights and fair wages?*

Key Principles of Ethical Consumerism:

- **Sustainability:** Choosing eco-friendly products that minimize environmental impact.

- **Fair Trade:** Supporting brands that ensure fair wages and humane working conditions.

- **Cruelty-Free Products:** Avoiding goods tested on animals.

- **Corporate Transparency:** Favoring businesses that disclose ethical practices.

- **Social Impact:** Supporting businesses that give back to communities.

---

2. How Ethical Consumerism is Changing Industries

Fashion: The Fall of Fast Fashion & Rise of Sustainable Brands

- The fast fashion industry ($2.5 trillion) has been exposed for exploiting workers, polluting the environment, and generating excessive waste.

- Ethical brands like **Patagonia, Everlane, and Reformation** are thriving because consumers demand **sustainability, fair wages, and transparency.**

- The **second-hand clothing market** (ThredUp, Poshmark) is growing, reducing waste and promoting circular fashion.

Food Industry: Fair Trade & Plant-Based Movements

- **Fair Trade Coffee & Chocolate:** Consumers are demanding fair wages for farmers, leading to widespread adoption of Fair Trade-certified products.

- **Plant-Based Boom:** Companies like **Beyond Meat**

and **Impossible Foods** are revolutionizing the food industry due to growing concerns about factory farming and climate change.

- **Organic & Sustainable Farming:** More consumers are choosing **organic, locally sourced, and non-GMO** food, forcing supermarkets and restaurants to adapt.

◻ **Beauty & Personal Care: Cruelty-Free and Sustainable Products**

- Major beauty brands like **Lush, The Body Shop, and Fenty Beauty** are thriving due to **cruelty-free, vegan, and sustainable** product lines.
- Consumer pressure led to **China lifting its mandatory animal testing requirement** for imported cosmetics in 2021.
- Brands like **Garnier and Dove** have reformulated products to eliminate harmful chemicals and reduce plastic waste.

◻ **Tech Industry: Demands for Transparency & Ethical Sourcing**

- **Apple & Tesla Face Pressure Over Ethical Sourcing:** Consumers demand **conflict-free minerals** (cobalt, lithium) and **fair labor conditions** in supply chains.
- **Privacy-Focused Products:** Growing demand for ethical data practices has led to **privacy-first alternatives** like **DuckDuckGo, ProtonMail, and Signal.**
- **E-Waste Solutions:** Brands like **Fairphone** are pioneering repairable, long-lasting smartphones to combat electronic waste.

3. The Power of Ethical Consumer Movements

Boycotts That Forced Corporate Change

Boycotts have been one of the most effective tools in ethical consumerism. When enough people withdraw their money, companies are forced to listen.

⬜ **Nike Sweatshop Scandal (1990s):** Widespread protests led to **better factory conditions and wage increases** for workers.

⬜ **Nestlé Baby Formula Controversy (1970s–Present):** Global boycotts forced Nestlé to improve marketing ethics regarding infant formula in developing nations.

⬜ **BP Oil Spill Backlash (2010):** Consumer pressure led to BP investing **$65 billion in environmental restoration.**

Sustainability Initiatives Driven by Consumer Demand

✓ **Starbucks & McDonald's Reducing Plastic Waste:** Following public pressure, both companies announced a shift to **biodegradable or reusable cups & straws.**

✓ **LEGO Going Green:** LEGO is investing in **plant-based and recycled plastic bricks** in response to consumer demands for sustainability.

✓ **Coca-Cola's Recyclable Packaging Commitment:** Coca-Cola pledged to **make 100% of its packaging recyclable by 2030.**

---

4. The Business Case for Ethical Consumerism

Many companies once believed ethical practices were "too expensive" or would hurt profits. However, the opposite has proven true:

⬜ **Sustainable brands outperform traditional brands.**

- Studies show that **66% of global consumers are willing to pay more for sustainable products.**

- The global market for **ethical fashion, organic food, and eco-friendly beauty** is growing faster than conventional markets.

- Companies like **Patagonia, Tesla, and Ben & Jerry's** have built billion-dollar businesses around ethical values.

☐ **Transparency Builds Trust & Customer Loyalty.**

- Brands that openly share **supply chain information, sustainability reports, and ethical initiatives** are gaining loyal customers.
- Younger generations (Millennials & Gen Z) are **more likely to boycott brands** that don't align with their values.

5. The Future of Ethical Consumerism

The rise of ethical consumerism shows no signs of slowing down. As more people become aware of their purchasing power, industries will continue to adapt. The next big shifts include:

☐ **Circular Economy Growth:** Companies will focus on reusable, repairable, and recyclable products to reduce waste.

☐ **Renewable Energy in Manufacturing:** More industries will transition to **solar, wind, and green energy sources** due to consumer pressure.

☐ **Ethical Tech & AI Regulations:** As AI and automation expand, consumers will demand **fair labor practices and ethical AI development.**

☐ **Greater Transparency in Supply Chains:** Blockchain and digital tracking will **expose unethical sourcing and allow consumers to make more informed choices.**

Final Thought: Your Money = Your Power

Ethical consumerism proves that **ordinary people have extraordinary influence.** Every purchase is a **statement about what kind of world you want to live in.**

Companies listen when profits are at stake. When consumers demand sustainability, fair wages, and humane practices, businesses adapt.

The next time you shop, ask yourself:
☐ *Is this product made ethically?*

☐ *Does this company align with my values?*
☐ *Am I supporting businesses that create positive change?*

Because **every dollar spent is a vote for the future.** What are you voting for?

CHAPTER 7: CASE STUDIES: HOW SMALL CONSUMER CHOICES LED TO MASSIVE CORPORATE SHIFTS

T hroughout history, consumer behavior has proven to be one of the most powerful forces for corporate change. While individual purchasing decisions may seem insignificant, when consumers unite behind a cause, their collective power can reshape entire industries. These case studies demonstrate how small consumer choices—boycotts, preferences, and ethical shopping—have forced major corporations to change their business models, labor practices, and environmental policies.

1. The Fall of Fast Fashion Giants – The Demand for Sustainable Clothing

☐ *Industry: Fashion & Apparel*
☐ *Impact: Shift from cheap, exploitative fast fashion to sustainable, ethical brands*

The Problem:

For decades, fast fashion brands like H&M, Zara, and Forever 21 built their success on mass-producing trendy, low-cost clothing. However, investigations exposed **exploitative labor conditions, environmental pollution, and massive textile waste.**

Consumer Action:

- Awareness campaigns and documentaries (e.g., *The True Cost*) educated people on **the dark side of fast fashion.**

- Consumers started **boycotting** unethical brands and choosing sustainable alternatives like **Patagonia, Everlane, and second-hand platforms like ThredUp.**

- Social media influencers promoted **minimalist fashion and "slow fashion" movements.**

Corporate Shift:

✓ **H&M launched its "Conscious Collection" and a garment recycling program.**
✓ **Zara committed to using 100% sustainable fabrics by 2025.**
✓ **Brands like Levi's reduced water waste and pledged ethical sourcing.**

Lesson:

When enough consumers **demand sustainability**, even the biggest fast fashion companies are forced to change their practices.

---

2. Starbucks & McDonald's Ditching Plastic Straws – The War on Plastic Waste

☐ *Industry: Food & Beverage*
☐ *Impact: Reduction of millions of plastic straws and packaging waste globally*

The Problem:

Plastic straws and packaging contribute to **ocean pollution,**

harming marine life and ecosystems. A viral video of a sea turtle with a plastic straw stuck in its nose sparked global outrage.

Consumer Action:

- Millions of people started **refusing plastic straws** and switching to **metal, bamboo, or paper alternatives.**
- Cities and governments imposed **plastic straw bans** due to public pressure.
- Social media campaigns like **#StopSucking and #PlasticFreeJuly** spread awareness.

Corporate Shift:

✓ **Starbucks committed to eliminating plastic straws globally by 2020.**
✓ **McDonald's phased out plastic straws in multiple countries, replacing them with biodegradable alternatives.**
✓ **Coca-Cola and Nestlé pledged to make all packaging recyclable by 2030.**

Lesson:

A simple consumer habit change—**refusing a plastic straw—triggered a global movement, forcing some of the world's biggest corporations to adapt.**

---

3. Nike & Adidas Forced to Address Sweatshop Labor Scandals

Industry: Sportswear & Footwear
Impact: Corporate transparency, higher wages, and improved labor conditions

The Problem:

In the 1990s, **Nike and Adidas were exposed for using sweatshops** in Asia, where workers—many of them children—were paid **pennies per hour** in **unsafe conditions.**

Consumer Action:

- Protests and **boycotts spread across universities and activist groups.**
- Celebrities and athletes refused to endorse brands linked to **child labor.**
- Ethical alternatives, like Fair Trade-certified shoes, gained popularity.

Corporate Shift:

✓ **Nike increased wages and improved factory working conditions.**
✓ **Adidas became one of the most transparent brands, releasing supply chain reports.**
✓ **Both brands pledged to use sustainable materials and reduce emissions.**

Lesson:

Public backlash and ethical shopping choices can **force billion-dollar corporations to prioritize human rights.**

---

4. The Rise of Plant-Based Meat – How Consumers Forced Fast-Food Chains to Change

☐ *Industry: Food & Agriculture*
☐ *Impact: Mainstream adoption of plant-based meat alternatives*

The Problem:

Factory farming is a leading cause of **deforestation, greenhouse gas emissions, and animal cruelty.** Traditional meat production is environmentally unsustainable.

Consumer Action:

- More people **adopted vegetarian and vegan diets** for ethical and environmental reasons.
- **Plant-based brands like Beyond Meat & Impossible Foods skyrocketed in sales.**
- Consumers demanded **more plant-based options in**

fast-food restaurants.

Corporate Shift:

✓ Burger King launched the Impossible Whopper.
✓ McDonald's introduced McPlant in multiple countries.
✓ KFC, Subway, and Dunkin' Donuts all added plant-based alternatives.

Lesson:

A small shift in eating habits **pushed even the biggest fast-food chains to rethink their menus.**

---

5. Fair Trade Coffee & Chocolate – Consumers Demand Ethical Sourcing

☐ *Industry: Food & Beverage*
☐ *Impact: Protection of farmers, elimination of child labor, and fair wages*

The Problem:

Major coffee and chocolate brands exploited farmers in **developing countries, paying extremely low wages while making billions in profit.** Many cacao farms used **child labor.**

Consumer Action:

- Ethical consumers **switched to Fair Trade-certified coffee and chocolate.**
- Public pressure forced brands to **prove they weren't using child labor.**
- Activists exposed corporations like Nestlé and Hershey for their supply chain violations.

Corporate Shift:

✓ Starbucks and Nestlé increased their Fair Trade sourcing.
✓ Hershey and Mars committed to 100% sustainable cocoa sourcing.
✓ Fair Trade chocolate brands (Divine, Tony's Chocolonely)

gained global market share.

Lesson:

When consumers demand **ethical sourcing, companies must adjust to stay relevant.**

---

6. Apple & Samsung Address Human Rights Issues in Tech Supply Chains

☐ *Industry: Technology & Electronics*
☐ *Impact: Greater transparency in supply chains and improved labor conditions*

The Problem:

Apple, Samsung, and other tech giants faced criticism for using minerals (cobalt, lithium) **sourced from mines with child labor and unethical working conditions.**

Consumer Action:

- People **demanded supply chain transparency.**
- Ethical tech alternatives like **Fairphone (a conflict-free smartphone) gained traction.**
- Governments and NGOs pressured companies to **audit their supply chains.**

Corporate Shift:

✓ **Apple committed to conflict-free mineral sourcing.**
✓ **Samsung introduced better labor monitoring systems.**
✓ **Fairphone became a model for sustainable smartphone production.**

Lesson:

Consumers have the power to push even tech giants toward **ethical and responsible manufacturing.**

Final Thought: Small Choices, Big Impact

These case studies prove a simple truth: **Consumers have**

enormous power. Every purchase decision, boycott, and ethical choice **shapes industries and forces corporations to change.**

When consumers demand:

◻ **Sustainable fashion** → **Brands reduce waste.**

◻ **Ethical coffee & chocolate** → **Farmers get fair wages.**

◻ **Plastic-free packaging** → **Companies stop using plastic.**

◻ **Cruelty-free beauty** → **Animal testing is banned.**

You don't need to be a CEO, billionaire, or politician to **change the world.**

You just need to choose where your money goes—because every dollar spent is a vote for the future. ◻◻

CHAPTER 8: THE POLITICAL INFLUENCE OF THE INDIVIDUAL

"A single vote, a single voice, and a single act of defiance have the power to change history."

Many people believe that political influence is reserved for politicians, activists, and the wealthy elite. This misconception leads to disengagement, allowing governments and institutions to operate without accountability. However, history has proven that individual citizens—through their votes, advocacy, and collective action—have the power to shape policies, overturn governments, and redefine societal values.

This chapter explores how **individuals influence political systems**, why every vote matters, and how grassroots movements have led to some of the most significant political changes in history.

1. Why Every Vote Matters More Than People Think

Many citizens feel that their vote is insignificant, but elections

—both local and national—are often decided by razor-thin margins.

☐ The Myth: "My Vote Won't Make a Difference"

- Many people believe that elections are predetermined, causing **low voter turnout** and making it easier for elites to maintain control.

- This mindset is particularly dangerous in **swing states or close elections**, where a few votes can determine policy direction for years.

☐ Historical Elections Decided by Just a Few Votes

☐ *US Presidential Election (2000):* **537 votes in Florida** decided the presidency, leading to the election of George W. Bush.

☐ *Brexit Referendum (2016):* A **51.9% to 48.1% split** changed the course of the UK forever.

☐ *Mexico Presidential Election (2006):* Won by a **0.56% margin**, sparking nationwide protests.

Lesson: When citizens don't vote, they let others decide their future.

---

2. The Rise of Grassroots Movements and Their Impact

Political power is not just in voting; **grassroots activism has led to some of the most important policy changes in history.**

☐ What Are Grassroots Movements?

- Movements started by **ordinary citizens** at the local level, often growing into national or global forces.

- They influence **laws, policies, and cultural attitudes** without relying on traditional political structures.

☐ Case Studies of Grassroots Power:

☐ Civil Rights Movement (USA, 1950s–60s)

- **Individuals like Rosa Parks sparked national change** by refusing to give up her bus seat.

- **Peaceful protests and activism** led to the Civil Rights Act of 1964, banning racial segregation.

☐ **Arab Spring (2010–2012, Middle East & North Africa)**

- Began when **Tunisian street vendor Mohamed Bouazizi** set himself on fire in protest of government corruption.
- Led to **the overthrow of governments** in Tunisia, Egypt, and Libya.

☐ **Fridays for Future (Climate Activism, 2018–Present)**

- Started by **Greta Thunberg**, a teenager protesting climate inaction.
- Grew into a **global youth-led movement**, pressuring governments to address climate change.

Lesson: Political revolutions don't start in government buildings—they start with citizens taking action.

---

3. How Citizens Can Influence Policy Beyond Voting

Many believe political engagement stops at voting, but **there are many ways individuals can shape policy and governance.**

☐ **Petitions and Citizen Advocacy**

- Online platforms like **Change.org and Avaaz** allow citizens to start petitions that gain millions of signatures.
- **Case Study: Stop SOPA & PIPA (2012)** – Online petitions and protests led to the defeat of controversial internet censorship laws.

☐ **Protests and Civil Disobedience**

- **Women's March (2017):** Millions protested against gender inequality and political oppression.
- **Black Lives Matter (2020):** Protests after George Floyd's death led to **police reforms, corporate**

commitments to diversity, and legal changes worldwide.

⬚ Holding Leaders Accountable

- **Contacting Representatives:** Phone calls, emails, and social media pressure **force politicians to address voter concerns.**

- **Media & Investigative Journalism:** Exposing corruption or political failures **forces governments to act.**

Lesson: Political power isn't just about elections—it's about continuous civic engagement.

---

4. Social Media as a Tool for Political Influence

Technology has revolutionized political participation. Today, **one viral post can reach millions, influence policy debates, and expose injustice.**

⬚ How Social Media Has Amplified Citizen Power

- **Twitter & Hashtag Movements:** #MeToo, #BlackLivesMatter, and #FridaysForFuture mobilized millions globally.

- **Citizen Journalism:** Smartphones and livestreaming have exposed police brutality, election fraud, and government abuse.

- **Digital Advocacy:** Activists now use TikTok, Instagram, and YouTube to educate, mobilize, and pressure leaders.

⬚ Case Study: The Power of Hashtags

⬚ **#MeToo Movement (2017-Present):** Millions of people shared stories of sexual harassment, leading to policy changes and legal action against abusers.

⬚ **#EndSARS (Nigeria, 2020):** Online activism exposed police brutality, forcing the Nigerian government to disband the controversial police unit.

Lesson: The internet has made political activism accessible to anyone with a smartphone.

---

5. The Future of Citizen-Led Political Influence

Political influence is evolving, and citizens have **more tools than ever** to hold leaders accountable.

◻ What's Next for Citizen Political Power?

◻ **Decentralized Politics:** Blockchain and AI may reduce corruption by making governance more transparent.
◻ **More Youth Engagement:** Younger generations are **more politically active than ever**, reshaping future policies.
◻ **Direct Democracy Movements:** More citizens are pushing for policies where **the people—not just politicians—directly vote on laws.**

Final Thought: Your Voice Shapes the Future

Political power does not belong **only to presidents, parliaments, or billionaires.** It belongs to **the people.**

◻ **If you don't vote, you let someone else decide your rights.**
◻ **If you don't speak out, you allow injustice to continue.**
◻ **If you don't act, you give up control over your future.**

Every movement that shaped history—from civil rights to climate action—**started with individuals who refused to remain silent.**

The question is not **whether you have political power.** The question is:

◻ **How will you use it?**

CHAPTER 9: WHY EVERY VOTE MATTERS MORE THAN PEOPLE REALIZE

"One vote may seem insignificant, but history has shown that elections, policies, and the future of nations can be decided by just a handful of ballots."

Many people believe that their vote doesn't matter—especially in large-scale elections where millions participate. However, this misconception is one of the greatest threats to democracy. In reality, elections, referendums, and policy decisions have been shaped by razor-thin margins, proving that every single vote counts.

This section explores **why voting is crucial, how elections have been decided by just a few votes, and how voter apathy allows elites to maintain control.**

1. The Myth: "My Vote Won't Make a Difference"

Many people don't vote because they believe:

- *"The system is rigged, so why bother?"*
- *"One vote won't change anything."*
- *"Politicians don't care about ordinary citizens."*

These false beliefs lead to **low voter turnout,** making it easier for special interest groups and politicians to **control elections with a smaller, more loyal base of voters.**

What Happens When People Don't Vote?

- Elections are decided by the **minority of people who do vote.**

- Politicians cater only to those who vote, ignoring those who stay silent.

- Corrupt or unqualified leaders win simply because **too many people chose not to participate.**

---

2. Historical Elections Decided by a Handful of Votes

If you think your vote doesn't matter, consider these real-world examples where just a few votes changed history:

US Presidential Election (2000) – **537 votes in Florida** decided the presidency, electing George W. Bush instead of Al Gore.

Brexit Referendum (2016, UK) – The vote to leave the European Union passed with **a margin of just 3.8% (51.9% to 48.1%),** changing the course of Britain's future forever.

Mexican Presidential Election (2006) – Felipe Calderón won by **a margin of just 0.56%,** leading to years of political unrest.

Senate Race in Minnesota (2008) – Al Franken won by just **312 votes,** giving Democrats a crucial 60-seat majority in the U.S. Senate.

Virginia House of Delegates (2017, USA) – The race ended in a tie, which was **decided by drawing a name from a bowl.** That single vote could have shifted legislative control in Virginia.

India General Elections (2014, 2019) – In many constituencies, candidates won by margins of **less than 500**

votes in a country of over 900 million eligible voters.

These examples show that **elections—whether local or national —can be decided by incredibly thin margins. One vote, one district, or one decision can change the entire direction of a country.**

3. The Power of Local Elections: Where Your Vote Has the Greatest Impact

While presidential or parliamentary elections get the most media attention, **local elections affect daily life more directly.**

 Why Local Elections Matter More Than People Realize

 Mayors & City Councils – Decide on public transportation, housing, schools, and policing.
 School Boards – Control education policies, budgets, and curriculum changes.
 State Legislators – Influence healthcare, wages, and environmental policies.
 Judges & Sheriffs – Make crucial legal and policing decisions that affect communities.

 Case Study: How Local Voting Changed a City

 Flint, Michigan Water Crisis (2014-Present)

- Local government decisions led to **lead contamination in the water supply, affecting thousands.**
- The mayor and city council members **who ignored the crisis were voted out in later elections.**
- If more people had voted **before** the crisis, better leaders might have prevented it.

4. How Voter Suppression and Apathy Benefit the Powerful

 Who Benefits When People Don't Vote?

 Wealthy elites – Fewer voters mean elections can be influenced with money and lobbying.

◻ **Corrupt politicians** – Lower turnout makes it easier for them to win without broad public support.
◻ **Special interest groups** – They gain more power when ordinary people don't participate.

◻ **Common Tactics Used to Suppress Voting**

◻ **Gerrymandering** – Politicians redraw district maps to favor their party.
◻ **Voter ID Laws** – Designed to discourage voting among marginalized communities.
◻ **Misinformation** – False claims about elections (e.g., "Your vote doesn't count" or "The election is rigged") discourage participation.

◻ **The Only Way to Fight Back: Vote in Large Numbers**

- The more people who vote, the harder it is for elites to manipulate results.
- Higher voter turnout **ensures that elections represent the true will of the people.**

---

5. The Ripple Effect: One Vote Can Change Policies for Decades

Elections don't just decide **who is in office**—they decide:
◻ **Healthcare Policies** – Whether public healthcare expands or gets cut.
◻ **Education Laws** – What students learn in school.
◻ **Climate Change Action** – If governments invest in clean energy or fossil fuels.
◻ **Worker Protections** – Whether wages, benefits, and labor rights improve.

◻ **Example: US Supreme Court Justices & Long-Term Policy Shifts**

- Presidents appoint **Supreme Court Justices**, who make **decisions affecting generations.**
- A single presidential election can determine **abortion rights, voting rights, and corporate regulations** for

decades.

- If **more young people and marginalized groups voted,** courts would reflect the broader population.

---

6. The Future of Voting: Making Every Vote Count

☐ **How Technology is Changing Elections**

☐ **Online Voter Registration** – More accessible for young and first-time voters.
☐ **Early Voting & Mail-in Ballots** – Expanding voting access beyond election day.
☐ **Blockchain Voting (Future Possibility)** – A secure, tamper-proof way to prevent election fraud.

☐ **The Role of Youth & First-Time Voters**

- **Younger generations** (Millennials & Gen Z) are **the largest voting bloc in history.**
- If they **turn out in high numbers,** they can reshape policies on **climate change, wages, and social justice.**
- Politicians will only prioritize **issues like student debt, healthcare, and fair wages** if young people vote consistently.

Final Thought: Your Vote is Your Power

When you don't vote, you're giving your power away.

☐ **One vote can change an election.**
☐ **One election can change a government.**
☐ **One government can change an entire nation.**

History is filled with examples of elections won by a **few hundred votes.** Policies that shape **your job, your healthcare, your rights, and your environment** are decided by who holds power.

The Question is Not "Does My Vote Matter?"—The Question is: "Will I Use My Power or Give it Away?"

The future is not decided by the politicians—it is decided by the voters. Be one of them.

CHAPTER 10: GRASSROOTS MOVEMENTS THAT OVERTURNED GOVERNMENTS

"When the people rise, even the most powerful governments can fall."

H istory has repeatedly shown that ordinary citizens, when united, have the power to bring down oppressive regimes, force policy changes, and reshape nations. Grassroots movements—political uprisings driven by everyday people—have played a crucial role in overturning governments and dictatorial rulers. These movements start small, often fueled by frustration, injustice, or economic hardship, but they grow into powerful forces that change the course of history.

This section highlights **some of the most impactful grassroots movements** that successfully challenged and overthrew governments, proving that **political power truly belongs to the** people.

1. The Arab Spring (2010–2012) – The Fall of Multiple Regimes

☐ Countries: Tunisia, Egypt, Libya, Yemen, Syria, Bahrain
☐ Impact: Overthrow of multiple dictatorships, democratic reforms, and civil unrest

How It Started:

- Sparked by a **single act of protest**—Tunisian street vendor **Mohamed Bouazizi set himself on fire** after being harassed by authorities.
- This act of defiance **ignited nationwide protests against corruption, unemployment, and dictatorship.**
- Protests quickly spread across the Middle East, fueled by **social media and mass demonstrations.**

Governments Overthrown:

☐ **Tunisia (2011):** President **Zine El Abidine Ben Ali** fled after 23 years in power.
☐ **Egypt (2011):** President **Hosni Mubarak**, who ruled for 30 years, resigned after mass protests.
☐ **Libya (2011):** Dictator **Muammar Gaddafi** was overthrown and killed after 42 years in power.
☐ **Yemen (2012):** President **Ali Abdullah Saleh** stepped down after massive demonstrations.

Lesson:

When **millions of citizens unite against injustice**, even the most powerful autocrats can be removed.

2. The Fall of the Berlin Wall (1989) – The Collapse of East Germany

☐ Country: Germany
☐ Impact: Fall of communist East Germany, reunification of

Germany

How It Started:

- For nearly **30 years, the Berlin Wall symbolized division and oppression**, separating East and West Germany.
- Citizens of East Germany were **denied freedom of movement, speech, and political rights.**
- Peaceful **Monday Demonstrations** began in Leipzig in 1989, **demanding political reforms and free elections.**

How the Government Collapsed:

- Protests grew from **a few hundred to over 500,000 people** in a matter of weeks.
- East German authorities **hesitated to use force**, fearing mass revolt.
- On **November 9, 1989**, overwhelmed by pressure, the government announced that **citizens were free to cross the wall.**

Lesson:

Nonviolent, persistent protests can **dismantle an entire government and reshape a nation.**

---

3. The People Power Revolution (1986) – Overthrowing a Dictator in the Philippines

☐ *Country: Philippines*
☐ *Impact: Fall of dictator Ferdinand Marcos, restoration of democracy*

How It Started:

- Ferdinand Marcos ruled the Philippines for **20 years under a corrupt, authoritarian regime.**
- After the **assassination of opposition leader Benigno Aquino Jr. in 1983**, public outrage grew.

- Citizens launched **mass protests, boycotts, and strikes** to challenge the dictatorship.

How the Government Fell:

- Over **two million Filipinos** took to the streets in **nonviolent protest.**
- The military **defected to the side of the people.**
- Marcos **fled the country**, and democracy was restored.

Lesson:

Even **peaceful, large-scale protests** can remove entrenched dictators without violence.

---

4. The Velvet Revolution (1989) – The End of Communist Rule in Czechoslovakia

☐ *Country: Czechoslovakia (Now Czech Republic & Slovakia)*
☐ *Impact: Fall of the communist regime, transition to democracy*

How It Started:

- For **40 years, Czechoslovakia was under Soviet-backed communist rule.**
- Inspired by **protests in East Germany and Poland,** Czech citizens began **nonviolent demonstrations.**
- The movement was **led by students, intellectuals, and workers demanding free elections.**

How the Government Fell:

- **Nationwide strikes and protests** escalated in November 1989.
- The government **refused to use military force**, fearing a full-scale revolution.
- By **December 1989**, the Communist Party resigned, and democracy was restored.

Lesson:

Civil resistance and **unity among citizens** can topple an oppressive government without a single shot being fired.

5. The Fall of Apartheid (1994) – Ending Racial Segregation in South Africa

☐ *Country: South Africa*
☐ *Impact: Overthrow of apartheid, first democratic elections, Nelson Mandela's presidency*

How It Started:

- Apartheid was a system of **racial segregation and white minority rule** that lasted for nearly 50 years.
- Citizens launched **grassroots resistance movements**, including boycotts, labor strikes, and global awareness campaigns.
- The **African National Congress (ANC), led by Nelson Mandela**, became the symbol of resistance.

How the Government Fell:

- **International economic sanctions** put immense pressure on the South African government.
- **Mass protests and strikes** weakened the apartheid regime.
- In **1994, Nelson Mandela was elected as South Africa's first Black president**, ending apartheid.

Lesson:

Decades of persistent grassroots activism can lead to the complete dismantling of systemic oppression.

6. The Ukrainian Orange Revolution (2004) – Overturning a Rigged Election

☐ *Country: Ukraine*
☐ *Impact: Overturning a fraudulent election, strengthening democracy*

How It Started:

- In **2004, presidential elections in Ukraine were widely believed to be rigged** in favor of pro-Russian candidate **Viktor Yanukovych.**

- Citizens launched **massive, peaceful protests,** demanding a new election.

- The movement became known as the **Orange Revolution** due to the symbolic color worn by protesters.

How the Government Fell:

- **Weeks of peaceful protests** in Kyiv forced the government to acknowledge election fraud.

- The **Supreme Court of Ukraine ordered a revote,** leading to the victory of opposition leader **Viktor Yushchenko.**

- The revolution **strengthened Ukraine's democracy** and weakened Russian influence.

Lesson:

Peaceful protests **can overturn election fraud** and protect democracy.

Final Thought: When the People Unite, Governments Fall

These grassroots movements prove one undeniable truth: **governments exist only with the consent of the governed.**

☐ **When citizens refuse to comply, corrupt leaders lose power.**
☐ **When people take to the streets, regimes collapse.**
☐ **When the silent majority rises, history is rewritten.**

The question is not whether ordinary people can change governments—the question is: Will they choose to act? ☐

CHAPTER 11: THE RIPPLE EFFECT OF CIVIC ENGAGEMENT

"One small act of civic participation can create waves of change across communities, societies, and even the world."

Many people underestimate the power of civic engagement—the simple act of participating in the democratic process, whether through voting, activism, or community service. What may seem like a small, individual action often has a ripple effect, influencing policy, inspiring others, and sparking larger movements.

Throughout history, countless examples demonstrate how **a single protest, a single vote, or a single voice** can initiate powerful societal change. This section explores how civic engagement, no matter how small, creates waves that **expand beyond the individual, influencing governments, businesses, and future generations.**

1. How Small Acts of Civic Engagement Create a Ripple Effect

Individual Actions Lead to Collective Movements

- When **one person speaks up**, it encourages others to do the same.

- Individual participation can **ignite grassroots activism**, leading to widespread change.

- **Example:** Rosa Parks' refusal to give up her bus seat in 1955 sparked the Montgomery Bus Boycott, a key moment in the Civil Rights Movement.

Local Engagement Leads to National Change

- Many major reforms start **at the local level** before spreading nationally or globally.

- **Example:** The fight for same-sex marriage in the U.S. began at the **state level**, with states like Massachusetts legalizing it before the Supreme Court ruling in 2015.

One Law or Policy Can Inspire Global Change

- When a country enacts a progressive law, it often inspires **other nations to follow suit.**

- **Example:** Sweden's carbon tax (introduced in 1991) inspired other governments to adopt similar policies to combat climate change.

---

2. Case Studies: The Ripple Effect in Action

The Civil Rights Movement (USA, 1950s–60s)

Ripple Effect: Inspired human rights movements worldwide.

- Small acts of civic engagement—**sit-ins, protests, and legal battles**—eventually led to major civil rights legislation.

- The movement inspired **anti-apartheid activists in South Africa**, and later **racial justice movements like Black Lives Matter.**

⬚ Greta Thunberg & the Youth Climate Movement (2018-Present)

Ripple Effect: One teenager's protest led to a global movement.

- Greta Thunberg started by **skipping school to protest climate inaction** in Sweden.
- Within months, her activism sparked **Fridays for Future**, a global youth movement with **millions of participants**.
- Governments worldwide **passed new climate laws**, companies pledged carbon neutrality, and climate action became a top political priority.

⬚ The Arab Spring (2010-2012)

Ripple Effect: A single act of defiance led to the fall of multiple dictatorships.

- Tunisian street vendor **Mohamed Bouazizi set himself on fire** in protest of police corruption.
- His act sparked **mass protests**, leading to the **overthrow of governments in Tunisia, Egypt, Libya, and Yemen**.
- The movement inspired **pro-democracy protests across the Middle East and North Africa**.

⬚ #MeToo Movement (2017-Present)

Ripple Effect: Transformed workplace policies worldwide.

- A single tweet exposing **sexual harassment in Hollywood** led to a global reckoning.
- The movement **changed workplace policies, laws, and public attitudes** on sexual misconduct.
- Powerful figures in politics, media, and business faced **legal action, resignations, and industry-wide reforms**.

3. How Civic Engagement Shapes Future Generations
☐ The Power of Role Models

- When one person **stands up for change**, it inspires others—especially young people—to do the same.
- **Example:** Malala Yousafzai's activism for girls' education encouraged millions to fight for educational rights worldwide.

☐ Community Involvement Strengthens Democracy

- Engaged citizens create **more accountable governments** and **better public policies.**
- **Example:** Participatory budgeting in Brazil allows citizens to decide how public funds are spent, leading to **reduced corruption and better services.**

☐ Each Generation Builds on the Last

- Movements that start in one era **pave the way for future progress.**
- **Example:** The feminist movements of the 20th century led to **gender equality laws** that today's activists continue to expand.

4. The Role of Digital Activism in Expanding Civic Engagement
☐ Social Media as a Political Tool

- Online activism **spreads awareness instantly** and mobilizes global support.
- **Example:** The Black Lives Matter protests were amplified through social media, leading to **policy changes, corporate commitments, and legal reforms.**

☐ Crowdfunding for Social Change

- Digital platforms allow **small donations to fund big**

movements.

- **Example:** GoFundMe campaigns have **covered medical expenses, legal battles, and community projects**, proving that small contributions add up to major impact.

 Digital Petitions & Online Organizing

- Websites like **Change.org and Avaaz** have enabled millions to **petition governments, corporations, and institutions** with just a few clicks.

---

5. How You Can Be Part of the Ripple Effect

✓ **Vote in Local & National Elections** – Your vote impacts policies that shape society.

✓ **Engage in Community Service** – Small local actions strengthen communities.

✓ **Educate & Share Information** – Conversations inspire awareness and change.

✓ **Support Ethical Businesses** – Consumer choices influence corporate policies.

✓ **Sign Petitions & Join Protests** – Collective action forces leaders to listen.

Final Thought: Every Action Creates Change

The world is not changed only by **politicians, billionaires, or celebrities**—it is shaped by **ordinary people taking small, consistent actions.**

 A single vote, a single voice, a single protest can create a ripple effect that transforms societies.

The question is not whether your engagement matters—**it's whether you choose to act.**

CHAPTER 12: THE CULTURAL IMPACT OF THE COMMON VOICE

"Culture is not shaped by elites—it is created by the voices, choices, and actions of ordinary people."

C ulture is the invisible force that binds societies together. It defines values, traditions, art, music, fashion, and even politics. While many believe that cultural shifts are dictated by governments, celebrities, or corporations, history proves that real cultural change starts with ordinary people.

Every movement that redefined a generation—civil rights, feminism, LGBTQ+ rights, environmentalism, and digital activism—began **not in boardrooms, but in homes, communities, and public spaces.** This chapter explores **how the voices of ordinary citizens** have shaped culture, influenced social norms, and redefined the future.

1. How Ordinary People Shape Culture

Culture is not static; it evolves based on the **collective actions and expressions of individuals.** Whether through art, social movements, or digital activism, **the everyday person has the power to redefine social norms and values.**

☐ **Social Norms and Behavior Change**

- **What is "normal" today was once radical.**
- Practices that were once accepted (e.g., segregation, gender discrimination) were challenged by **citizens demanding progress.**
- **Example:** Smoking was once a cultural norm. Grassroots health campaigns led to a decline in smoking rates worldwide.

☐ **Everyday Actions That Change Perceptions**

- **Language evolves** based on common usage (e.g., gender-neutral terms becoming widely accepted).
- **Fashion trends** are dictated by youth culture, street style, and countercultural movements, not just designers.
- **Consumer habits** (like buying local or ethical brands) push industries to change their approach.

☐ **Cultural Revolutions Led by the Common Voice**

☐ **The Renaissance (14th–17th Century):** Artists, writers, and philosophers—not kings—sparked a new era of art and thought.
☐ **The Civil Rights Movement (1960s):** Marches, sit-ins, and grassroots activism reshaped racial attitudes and policies.
☐ **The LGBTQ+ Rights Movement:** Ordinary people coming out and advocating for rights led to global acceptance and policy changes.

2. The Role of Social Movements in Cultural Change

Social movements are **the heartbeat of cultural transformation.** They challenge oppressive norms and introduce **new ways of thinking.**

☐ **Case Study: Feminism & Women's Rights**

- The suffrage movement (19th–20th century) won women the right to vote.
- The **#MeToo movement (2017)** started as a hashtag and became a **global reckoning against sexual harassment.**
- Women in **Saudi Arabia gained the right to drive (2018)** after grassroots activism and international pressure.

⬛ Case Study: The Digital Age & Cancel Culture

- Social media has given ordinary people **the power to hold the powerful accountable.**
- The rise of **"cancel culture"** has reshaped public discourse on ethics, celebrity behavior, and corporate responsibility.
- **Example:** The downfall of Harvey Weinstein due to social media exposure led to systemic changes in Hollywood.

⬛ Case Study: The Environmental Movement

- Rachel Carson's book *Silent Spring* (1962) sparked **global environmental consciousness.**
- Greta Thunberg's school strike inspired **millions of young activists worldwide.**
- Public demand for sustainability has forced brands like **Nike, Apple, and Tesla** to commit to greener practices.

---

3. How Music, Art, and Media Reflect the Power of the Common Voice

⬛ Music as a Protest Tool

- **Hip-hop, punk, folk, and reggae** have all been tools for **political and social resistance.**
- **Examples:**
  - Bob Dylan's songs fueled the civil rights

movement.

- ◦ Hip-hop in the 1990s spoke against police brutality and systemic racism.
- ◦ Reggae (e.g., Bob Marley) became a voice for anti-colonialism and peace.

☐ Art & Film as Cultural Weapons

- **Street art and graffiti** (e.g., Banksy, Shepard Fairey) have **challenged authority and spread activist messages.**

- Films like *Black Panther* and *Parasite* highlighted issues of race and class inequality, **sparking global conversations.**

- **Documentaries** (*13th, An Inconvenient Truth*) have educated the public and pressured policymakers.

☐ The Power of Independent Media

- Traditional media was once controlled by a few networks, but today, **citizen journalism and independent platforms challenge the mainstream narrative.**

- **YouTube, podcasts, and blogs** have empowered everyday people to tell **real, unfiltered stories.**

- **Example:** The George Floyd protests gained momentum through social media live-streaming, **proving the power of citizen reporting.**

4. The Internet & Social Media: The Amplification of the Common Voice

☐ The Digital Age Has Democratized Influence

- In the past, only **newspapers, TV stations, and governments controlled information.**

- Today, **anyone with a smartphone can shape public opinion.**

- Movements like **#MeToo**, **#BLM**, **and #FridaysForFuture** spread worldwide without traditional media backing.

Viral Campaigns That Changed the World

#IceBucketChallenge (2014): Raised **$115 million** for ALS research.

#BlackLivesMatter (2013–Present): Shifted global conversations on racism and police reform.

#EndSARS (Nigeria, 2020): Exposed police brutality and led to major reforms.

Crowdsourced Activism & Fundraising

- GoFundMe and Kickstarter have **enabled ordinary people to fund social causes, businesses, and medical treatments.**

- Crowdsourced bail funds have helped protestors, refugees, and activists.

5. Cultural Resistance: When Governments & Corporations Push Back

Governments Attempt to Control Culture

- Authoritarian regimes often **ban books, censor the internet, and control the media** to suppress independent voices.

- **Example:** China's censorship of pro-democracy content and social media restrictions.

Corporate Influence on Culture

- Large corporations **try to shape consumer culture** through advertising and branding.

- But **public pressure has forced companies to be more socially responsible** (e.g., Nike supporting Colin Kaepernick's racial justice activism).

The People Always Find a Way to Resist

- Even in dictatorships, underground music, literature, and art continue to **challenge oppression.**
- Social media and VPNs allow activists to bypass censorship.
- **Example:** Protesters in Hong Kong used **encrypted messaging apps** to organize demonstrations.

6. The Future of Cultural Influence: Where Do We Go from Here?

- **Decentralized Media:** Independent creators and platforms will continue to disrupt traditional media monopolies.
- **Activist Brands:** Companies will be forced to align with social causes or face backlash.
- **Global Youth Influence:** Gen Z and Millennials are the most politically engaged generations, shaping the future of culture.

Final Thought: Culture Belongs to the People

⬜ **Ordinary people shape culture more than politicians or corporations ever could.**

⬜ **What we consume, share, support, and protest defines the world we live in.**

⬜ **From social movements to viral hashtags, culture is built from the bottom up—not the top down.**

The question isn't **whether you influence culture—it's how you choose to do it.**

⬜ **Will you be a passive consumer, or will you be an active voice in shaping the world?** ⬜⬜⬜

CHAPTER 13: HOW SOCIAL MEDIA GAVE POWER TO EVERYDAY VOICES

"In the digital age, one tweet, one post, or one video can spark a movement, expose injustice, and change the world."

Social media has revolutionized communication, activism, and influence, shifting power away from traditional media, governments, and corporations and placing it directly in the hands of ordinary people. Unlike in the past, when information was controlled by a select few, social media allows anyone with an internet connection to share their thoughts, expose corruption, and mobilize millions.

This section explores how social media has empowered everyday voices, fueled political and social movements, and forced institutions to respond to the collective power of citizens.

1. The Democratization of Influence

Before social media, influence was controlled by:

□ **Television Networks** – Only a few media companies decided what stories were told.

□ **Newspapers & Magazines** – Journalists and editors dictated public opinion.

□ **Politicians & Corporations** – Those with money and power controlled narratives.

□ **How Social Media Changed Everything**

- **Anyone** can now share their thoughts, breaking the monopoly of traditional media.

- **Real-time reporting** has exposed corruption and human rights violations faster than ever.

- **Movements that once took years to build can now gain traction overnight.**

□ **Case Study: Citizen Journalism Exposes Police Brutality**

- Before smartphones, police brutality was often ignored or dismissed.

- **In 2020, a 17-year-old, Darnella Frazier, recorded the murder of George Floyd,** sparking global protests.

- The **video went viral**, forcing police accountability and legislative changes.

2. Viral Hashtags That Changed the World

Hashtags have become **digital rallying cries**, organizing global conversations and movements.

□ **#MeToo (2017-Present)** – Sparked a worldwide reckoning on sexual harassment and workplace abuse.

□ **#BlackLivesMatter (2013-Present)** – Brought attention to systemic racism and police brutality.

□ **#FridaysForFuture (2018-Present)** – Inspired millions to demand climate action.

□ **#EndSARS (2020, Nigeria)** – Exposed police brutality, leading to government reforms.

▯ **#IceBucketChallenge (2014)** – Raised **$115 million** for ALS research through viral participation.

▯ **The Power of a Single Hashtag**

- **#MeToo** started with a few women sharing their stories—within days, it became a global movement.

- **#FridaysForFuture** began with **one teenage girl, Greta Thunberg**, skipping school to protest climate inaction; today, millions have joined.

- **#EndSARS** led to street protests and forced the Nigerian government to disband the Special Anti-Robbery Squad (SARS).

▯ **Lesson:** One tweet, one story, or one post can **ignite global change.**

---

3. The Rise of Digital Activism

Social media has transformed **how people organize protests, share information, and demand accountability.**

▯ **How Activists Use Social Media to Organize Movements**

- **Twitter & Instagram:** Spread awareness and coordinate events.

- **Facebook Groups:** Allow people to mobilize within local communities.

- **TikTok & YouTube:** Share personal stories and expose injustices.

▯ **Case Study: The Arab Spring (2010-2012)**

- Protesters used **Facebook & Twitter** to **coordinate demonstrations against oppressive regimes.**

- Videos of government violence were **shared instantly**, exposing corruption.

- The movement led to the **overthrow of multiple**

dictators, proving the power of digital activism.

⬜ **Lesson:** Social media can be more powerful than traditional political organizing.

---

4. Holding Corporations & Governments Accountable

Social media gives **ordinary people the power to challenge those in power.**

⬜ **Examples of Social Media Pressure Leading to Real Change**

⬜ **Nike & Sweatshops (1990s-Present):** Consumer backlash forced Nike to reform labor practices.

⬜ **Pepsi & Tone-Deaf Advertising (2017):** Social media outrage led Pepsi to pull an ad featuring Kendall Jenner.

⬜ **United Airlines Scandal (2017):** Viral video of a passenger being forcibly removed caused **United Airlines' stock to drop by $1 billion in a day.**

⬜ **Lesson:** Companies and governments **fear public backlash,** giving consumers unprecedented power.

---

5. The Future of Social Media & Citizen Power

⬜ **What's Next?**

⬜ **Decentralized Platforms** – New networks may challenge the dominance of Facebook, Twitter, and YouTube.

⬜ **More Transparency** – Calls for ethical AI and fact-checking to combat misinformation.

⬜ **Greater Citizen Journalism** – Everyday people will continue to expose injustices through digital media.

⬜ **The Challenges of Social Media Power**

⬜ **Misinformation & Fake News** – False stories spread just as fast as real ones.

⬜ **Censorship & Algorithm Control** – Tech giants decide what people see, raising concerns over free speech.

⬜ **Government Crackdowns** – Some nations (e.g., China, Iran) have banned social media to silence dissent.

◻ **Lesson:** The **power of social media is only as strong as the people who use it wisely.**

Final Thought: Social Media is the Megaphone of the Common Voice

◻ **Ordinary people now have a global platform to challenge corruption, demand change, and create movements.**

◻ **Hashtags have become digital protest banners, and viral videos have become evidence for justice.**

◻ **The power of information is no longer in the hands of the elite—it's in the hands of the people.**

The question isn't whether your voice can be heard. The question is: What will you do with it?

CHAPTER 14:
THE ROLE OF
ORDINARY CITIZENS
IN CULTURAL
REVOLUTIONS

"Cultural revolutions are not started by governments, corporations, or elites—they are built by the people, for the people."

C ulture is constantly evolving, and history proves that ordinary citizens are the true architects of cultural revolutions. Whether through art, music, literature, fashion, activism, or social movements, everyday people have challenged oppressive norms, redefined values, and reshaped societies.

From the Renaissance to the Civil Rights Movement, from LGBTQ+ rights to the rise of the digital age, cultural revolutions have always been fueled by **grassroots activism, community engagement, and the courage of individuals who refuse to**

accept the status quo.

This section explores **how ordinary citizens have played a crucial role in cultural revolutions**, proving that real change always starts from the bottom up.

---

1. What is a Cultural Revolution?

A **cultural revolution** is a **fundamental shift in societal norms, values, and traditions** driven by widespread participation. It affects how people think, behave, and express themselves.

 Key Characteristics of Cultural Revolutions

✓ **They challenge traditional norms** – People reject outdated beliefs and demand change.
✓ **They are driven by ordinary citizens** – Not politicians or corporations, but artists, students, activists, and workers.
✓ **They reshape multiple aspects of society** – Politics, economy, fashion, music, gender roles, and social structures.
✓ **They often face resistance before acceptance** – Many cultural revolutions begin as radical movements before becoming mainstream.

---

2. Historical Examples of Cultural Revolutions Led by Ordinary People

 The Renaissance (14th-17th Century) – A Shift in Art, Science, and Philosophy

 Who Led It? – Artists, writers, and scientists—not kings or religious leaders.
 Impact:

- Ordinary artists like **Leonardo da Vinci and Michelangelo** redefined art and architecture.
- Thinkers like **Galileo and Copernicus** challenged the Catholic Church's control over science.
- Printing presses allowed **common people to access books**, spreading revolutionary ideas.

 Lesson: A handful of artists, scholars, and citizens **sparked an intellectual and artistic explosion that shaped modern Europe.**

 The Industrial Workers' Movements (19th-20th Century) – Changing Labor Laws

 Who Led It? – Factory workers, trade unions, and everyday laborers.

 Impact:

- **Child labor laws, minimum wage, and the 8-hour workday** became standard.
- **Unions and strikes** forced business owners to improve working conditions.
- **Worker rights movements spread worldwide,** shaping labor policies for future generations.

 Lesson: Ordinary workers fought for—and won—the labor rights we take for granted today.

 The Civil Rights Movement (1950s-60s) – Ending Racial Segregation

 Who Led It? – Students, teachers, churchgoers, and everyday citizens.

 Impact:

- Sit-ins, bus boycotts, and nonviolent protests **forced legal changes against segregation.**
- People like **Rosa Parks and Martin Luther King Jr.** became leaders, but the movement was built by **millions of ordinary people.**
- Led to the **Civil Rights Act of 1964,** transforming racial equality in the U.S.

 Lesson: Cultural revolutions need mass participation, not just a few leaders.

◻ The Feminist Movements (20th-21st Century) – Women Demanding Equality

◻ *Who Led It?* – Writers, students, activists, and working-class women.

◻ *Impact:*

- **The suffrage movement** led to women gaining the right to vote.
- **The workplace equality movement** forced changes in hiring and wage policies.
- **The #MeToo movement** challenged sexual harassment in workplaces worldwide.

◻ **Lesson:** Women's rights movements started **at kitchen tables and college campuses before reaching global platforms.**

◻ The LGBTQ+ Rights Movement – From Criminalization to Acceptance

◻ *Who Led It?* – Ordinary LGBTQ+ individuals, grassroots activists, and allies.

◻ *Impact:*

- **The Stonewall Riots (1969),** led by drag queens, trans women, and gay activists, sparked a revolution.
- The first **Pride parades** were organized by citizens, not politicians.
- Decades of activism led to **legalized same-sex marriage** in dozens of countries.

◻ **Lesson:** What started as a **marginalized movement became a mainstream cultural shift** due to the persistence of ordinary people.

---

3. How Modern Technology Accelerates Cultural Revolutions

In the past, cultural revolutions took **decades or even centuries** to spread. Today, **social media and digital activism** allow ordinary people to challenge societal norms in real-time.

☐ The Role of Digital Activism

- **#MeToo exposed workplace harassment** across industries.
- **#BlackLivesMatter reshaped global conversations on race and police brutality.**
- **The Arab Spring used social media** to organize protests and overthrow dictators.

☐ **Lesson:** Digital platforms have given **ordinary people the power to influence global culture faster than ever before.**

---

4. The Role of Artists, Musicians, and Writers in Cultural Change

Music, art, and literature **have always been tools for cultural revolution.** They challenge the status quo and spread ideas in ways that speeches and laws cannot.

☐ Music as a Voice for Change

☐ **Bob Dylan's songs fueled the Civil Rights Movement.**
☐ **Punk music challenged political corruption and social norms.**
☐ **Hip-hop gave a voice to marginalized communities, exposing racial injustice.**

☐ Art as Resistance

☐ **Graffiti and street art (e.g., Banksy) highlight social issues and government corruption.**
☐ **Political cartoons have historically criticized leaders and influenced public opinion.**

☐ **Lesson:** Cultural revolutions **begin in art, music, and literature before becoming mainstream change.**

---

5. How You Can Contribute to Cultural Change

Not every cultural revolution needs mass protests—**small actions create ripple effects that influence future generations.**

✓ **Speak out against injustice** in everyday conversations.

✓ **Support independent artists and creators** who challenge societal norms.

✓ **Share and amplify movements** that push for equality, sustainability, and human rights.

✓ **Educate yourself and others** about history, politics, and cultural shifts.

✓ **Use social media to spread awareness** about causes you believe in.

☐ **Lesson:** You don't have to be famous or powerful to contribute —**your actions shape the future of culture.**

Final Thought: Culture Belongs to the People

☐ **Every cultural revolution in history started with ordinary citizens who refused to conform.**

☐ **The way you think, act, and speak contributes to shaping societal values.**

☐ **Your choices today define the culture of tomorrow.**

The question is not whether you influence culture—it's how you choose to do it.

CHAPTER 15: EXAMPLES: MUSIC, FILMS, BOOKS, AND SOCIAL TRENDS DRIVEN BY NON-ELITES

"The most powerful cultural shifts have not come from kings, politicians, or billionaires—they have come from ordinary people expressing their realities through music, films, books, and movements."

C ulture is often shaped from the ground up, rather than dictated by the elite. Some of the most impactful songs, films, literature, and social trends that changed history, challenged authority, and inspired movements came from working-class artists, activists, and everyday people.

This section highlights key examples of **music, films, books,**

and social trends that were driven by **non-elites**—ordinary individuals who created works that **reshaped society, politics, and cultural norms.**

1. Music as a Tool for Revolution

Music has long been a **powerful weapon for social change**, giving a voice to **oppressed communities, protest movements, and marginalized groups.** Many of the most revolutionary songs were not created by the wealthy or politically connected, but by **working-class musicians, immigrants, and activists.**

☐ **Folk & Protest Songs (1960s – Civil Rights & Anti-War Movements)**

☐ **Bob Dylan – "Blowin' in the Wind" (1962)** – Became an anthem for the **civil rights movement and anti-Vietnam War protests.**
☐ **Sam Cooke – "A Change is Gonna Come" (1964)** – A deeply personal song about **racial injustice and hope for a better future.**

☐ **Hip-Hop & Rap (1970s-Present – A Voice for Marginalized Communities)**

☐ **Grandmaster Flash – "The Message" (1982)** – Exposed the struggles of **poverty and crime in Black communities** in New York.
☐ **Public Enemy – "Fight the Power" (1989)** – A protest song against **racial injustice and police brutality.**
☐ **Tupac Shakur – "Changes" (1998)** – Tackled issues of **racism, poverty, and systemic oppression.**

☐ **Punk Rock (1970s-1980s – Challenging Authority & Capitalism)**

☐ **The Clash – "London Calling" (1979)** – Criticized **political corruption and economic inequality.**
☐ **Dead Kennedys – "Holiday in Cambodia" (1980)** – Mocked **Western hypocrisy and political apathy.**

☐ **Lesson:** Music created by ordinary people **has the power to** inspire revolutions and challenge oppressive systems.

2. Films That Started Conversations & Challenged Society

Films have often been a **catalyst for social change,** sparking debates about race, gender, war, and inequality. Some of the most impactful films were created **outside the Hollywood elite** and came from independent filmmakers or working-class directors.

Films That Challenged Racial Inequality

 "12 Years a Slave" (2013) – Told the true story of **Solomon Northup, a free Black man kidnapped into slavery.**
 "Moonlight" (2016) – A small, independent film that **broke stereotypes about Black masculinity and LGBTQ+ identity.**

Films That Criticized Capitalism & Class Struggles

 "Parasite" (2019) – A South Korean film made by non-Hollywood filmmakers that **exposed class divisions and economic inequality.**
 "Sorry to Bother You" (2018) – A dark comedy about **corporate greed, racism, and labor exploitation.**

Independent Films That Changed LGBTQ+ Representation

 "Boys Don't Cry" (1999) – Based on the real-life story of **Brandon Teena, a trans man murdered in a hate crime.**
 "The Handmaiden" (2016) – A South Korean film that broke **barriers for LGBTQ+ representation in cinema.**

 Lesson: Independent films by non-elites **have reshaped global conversations about race, gender, and inequality.**

3. Books That Sparked Movements

Books written by **ordinary people—activists, journalists, and self-taught authors—**have played a key role in **political revolutions, civil rights, and feminist movements.** Many of these books were initially rejected by elites but later **became essential reading for generations of activists.**

Books That Challenged Oppression & Injustice

"The Diary of Anne Frank" (1947) – A firsthand account of the Holocaust from a teenage girl hiding from the Nazis.

"I Know Why the Caged Bird Sings" (1969) – Maya Angelou – A memoir about **racism, sexism, and Black womanhood in America.**

Books That Fueled Feminist Movements

"The Feminine Mystique" (1963) – Betty Friedan – Ignited second-wave feminism by challenging traditional gender roles.

"Women, Race & Class" (1981) – Angela Davis – Explored the intersection of feminism, racism, and class oppression.

Books That Sparked Anti-Colonial & Social Justice Movements

"Pedagogy of the Oppressed" (1968) – Paulo Freire – Inspired education reforms in Latin America, Africa, and beyond.

"The Wretched of the Earth" (1961) – Frantz Fanon – Became a guidebook for anti-colonial resistance in Africa.

Lesson: Books written by **activists, refugees, and marginalized voices** have shaped major political and social movements.

---

4. Social Trends & Grassroots Movements Led by Ordinary People

Culture isn't just shaped by artists and writers—**everyday people create trends that change the way we live, dress, and think.**

The DIY Movement & Indie Culture

- The **punk subculture (1970s)** created the **DIY (Do It Yourself) ethic,** where independent musicians, artists, and designers refused corporate influence.

- The rise of **indie publishing, self-released music,**

and handmade crafts empowered creators outside of mainstream industries.

☐ **The Vegan & Ethical Consumerism Movements**

- What started as **a niche movement in the 1970s** became a **global trend**, forcing companies like McDonald's and Nestlé to offer **plant-based alternatives**.
- Ethical shopping—choosing Fair Trade, local businesses, and second-hand fashion—**gained popularity thanks to grassroots activism**.

☐ **The Rise of Social Media Activism**

- **#BlackLivesMatter (2013-present)** began as a hashtag and **became a global movement** fighting systemic racism.
- **#MeToo (2017-present)** started as individual women sharing their stories and **led to changes in corporate and legal policies**.

☐ **Lesson:** Everyday people **start the cultural trends that shape industries, politics, and economies.**

Final Thought: Culture Belongs to the People

☐ **Music, films, books, and social trends are shaped by ordinary citizens—not elites.**

☐ **Every major cultural revolution began with individuals speaking out against injustice.**

☐ **If you want to change the world, start with your voice, your art, your choices.**

The question isn't whether ordinary people shape culture—the question is, how will YOU shape it? ☐☐☐

PART THREE: THE CHALLENGES FACING THE ORDINARY CITIZEN

CHAPTER 16: THE SYSTEM'S CONTROL OVER THE INDIVIDUAL

"The greatest trick the system ever pulled was convincing people they have no power."

From the moment we are born, we are shaped by political, economic, and social systems that dictate how we live, think, and behave. Governments, corporations, and media industries control information, limit opportunities, and manipulate perception to maintain their power. The result? A passive, compliant population that rarely questions the status quo.

This chapter examines **how the system controls individuals, the tactics used to keep citizens powerless, and what can be done to break free.**

1. The Illusion of Choice: How Power Structures Limit Freedom

Many people believe they are free because they can **vote, shop, and express opinions online.** But true freedom means more than just participating in a system—it means having the power to **shape the system itself.**

☐ **How the Illusion Works**

- **Controlled Elections** – Most political choices are between **candidates backed by the same corporate interests.**

- **Consumerism as a Distraction** – People are encouraged to focus on **buying products rather than demanding systemic change.**

- **Education System Conditioning** – Schools teach **obedience and memorization** rather than **critical thinking and activism.**

☐ **Example: The Two-Party System in Many Countries**

- Voters believe they have a **choice,** but both major political parties **serve corporate interests and maintain the status quo.**

- Third parties and independent voices are often **silenced or ignored by mainstream media.**

☐ **Lesson:** True choice comes when **people demand systemic changes, not just different faces within the same system.**

---

2. Media & Propaganda: How Information is Manipulated

☐ **Who Controls the News?**

- **90% of the world's media is owned by a handful of corporations.**

- News is often **filtered** to protect political and corporate interests.

- Sensationalism and fear-based reporting keep **people distracted and divided.**

☐ **The Rise of "Fake News" & Misinformation**

- Governments and corporations use **disinformation campaigns** to confuse and divide the public.

- **Example:** During elections, **social media bots spread false information** to manipulate voter behavior.
- Historical events are often **rewritten** to serve political narratives.

How Social Media Algorithms Control Thought

- Algorithms **prioritize engagement over truth**, meaning **misleading content spreads faster than factual reporting.**
- **Echo chambers** keep people locked in **one-sided perspectives, preventing real debate.**

Lesson: Seek independent sources, question everything, and recognize when media is shaping emotions rather than informing.

---

3. Economic Control: How Financial Systems Keep People Dependent

The Wealth Gap & Systemic Poverty

- The world's richest **1% own more wealth than 99% of the population.**
- Wages **haven't kept up with inflation**, making economic mobility harder.
- **Student debt, credit loans, and mortgage systems** are designed to keep people financially trapped.

How Debt is Used as a Tool of Control

- **Low wages and high costs** keep workers too busy struggling for survival to engage in activism.
- **Example:** Many people work **multiple jobs** just to cover rent and healthcare, leaving no time for civic engagement.

Lesson: Financial literacy and **economic independence** are key to breaking free from systemic control.

---

4. Fear & Compliance: How Governments Keep Populations Passive

 Fear as a Political Tool

- Governments use **fear-based narratives** to justify increased control.
- **Example:** "War on Terror" policies led to **mass surveillance and loss of privacy.**

 The Criminalization of Dissent

- Protesters, whistleblowers, and activists are **labeled as threats** to national security.
- Laws are passed to **silence opposition and discourage collective action.**
- **Example:** Many countries have laws that restrict **mass protests and online activism.**

 Lesson: Awareness is the first step. Recognizing fear tactics helps individuals resist psychological manipulation.

---

5. How to Break Free from Systemic Control

✓ **Educate Yourself & Others**

- Read **independent journalism** and **books banned by governments and corporations.**
- Learn about **economic structures, propaganda tactics, and psychological manipulation.**

✓ **Build Financial Independence**

- Reduce reliance on **corporate banks and debt-based lifestyles.**
- Support **local businesses, cooperative enterprises, and ethical investments.**

✓ **Resist Fear-Based Narratives**

- Question laws and policies that **limit freedoms in the**

name of security.

- **Support whistleblowers** who expose corruption.

✓ **Organize & Take Action**

- Join **grassroots movements** that challenge oppressive systems.

- **Vote strategically** and push for **electoral reforms** that reduce corporate influence.

Final Thought: The System Only Works if You Comply

 The greatest fear of those in power is an informed, united, and financially independent population.

 Every system of control—political, economic, and media—is designed to make you feel powerless.

 But once you see through the illusion, you can start reclaiming your autonomy.

The question isn't whether the system controls you—the question is, will you fight back?

CHAPTER 17: HOW CORPORATIONS AND GOVERNMENTS MANIPULATE PERCEPTIONS

"If you control what people see, hear, and believe, you control what they do."

B oth corporations and governments have mastered the art of manipulating public perception to maintain power, suppress dissent, and maximize profits. By controlling media narratives, education, advertising, and even social movements, they shape public opinion, manufacture consent, and prevent collective resistance.

This chapter explores **the key tactics used by powerful institutions to control perception** and how ordinary citizens can recognize and resist these manipulations.

---

1. Controlling the Narrative: How Media is Used to Shape

Perception

Most people believe that the **news provides an objective reality.** In truth, **the media is often owned, funded, or influenced by powerful corporations and governments** that use it to manipulate public opinion.

☐ **Who Owns the Media?**

- **90% of all news outlets in the U.S. are controlled by just five corporations:** Comcast, Disney, Warner Bros. Discovery, Paramount, and Fox.

- Globally, media is often controlled by **government-funded networks or billionaire-owned conglomerates.**

- These companies control **what gets reported, how issues are framed, and what is ignored.**

☐ **Tactics Used to Control the Media**

☐ **Selective Coverage** – Certain stories are **amplified** while others are buried.

☐ **Framing Bias** – The same event is portrayed differently depending on the agenda.

☐ **Distraction Tactics** – Celebrity scandals or sensationalized stories dominate the news cycle, keeping people from focusing on real issues.

☐ **Example: War Propaganda & Media Manipulation**

- **The Iraq War (2003):** U.S. media repeatedly pushed the false narrative of **"weapons of mass destruction"**, leading to public support for an unnecessary war.

- **Rwanda Genocide (1994):** The global media largely ignored the crisis until it was too late, allowing atrocities to continue.

☐ **Lesson:** Media doesn't always "report" events—it often **creates** public perception of them.

2. Psychological Manipulation: The Science of Public Control

Governments and corporations use **psychological tactics** to shape public perception **without people even realizing it.**

The Use of Fear & Crisis to Control Populations

- Fear is the **most effective tool for social control.** When people are afraid, they seek **authority and protection, making them more likely to accept restrictions on freedom.**

- Governments use crises—**wars, terrorism, pandemics**—to justify surveillance, censorship, and greater police powers.

- **Example:** After 9/11, the U.S. government passed the **Patriot Act**, expanding mass surveillance while telling citizens it was "for their protection."

Divide & Conquer: How Elites Prevent Unity

- Citizens are **intentionally divided** by race, class, religion, and political ideology so they never unite against real oppressors.

- **Example:** Politicians focus on **cultural issues (abortion, religion, race debates)** to keep people distracted from **corporate tax cuts and economic inequality.**

Lesson: If the system keeps you in fear, divided, and distracted —it's by design.

---

3. Corporations & The Illusion of Free Choice

Most people believe they have **freedom of choice** as consumers. In reality, our choices are **carefully engineered by corporate influence.**

The Illusion of Market Competition

- **Most major industries are monopolized**—a handful of corporations control most brands.

- **Example:**
  - PepsiCo owns **Lay's, Tropicana, Gatorade, Quaker, and Cheetos.**
  - Nestlé owns **over 2,000 brands**, including **Gerber, KitKat, Nescafé, and Poland Spring.**
  - **Amazon dominates online retail**, giving the illusion of small businesses while controlling most sales.

☐ **Planned Obsolescence: Keeping Consumers Trapped in Endless Spending**

- Products are **designed to break down** so consumers **must keep buying replacements.**
- **Example:** Apple **intentionally slows down older iPhones** to force users to upgrade.

☐ **Advertising & Behavioral Manipulation**

- The advertising industry **spends billions to shape consumer desires** through psychological triggers.
- Corporations **sell insecurity**, making people feel inadequate without their products.
- **Example:** The beauty industry profits from **body image issues** it helps create through marketing.

☐ **Lesson:** If corporations can control what you **desire**, they can control your **spending.**

---

4. Social Media & Algorithmic Control

While social media has given individuals a voice, **corporations and governments still control what people see.**

☐ **How Algorithms Manipulate Reality**

- **Social media platforms are designed to keep users addicted.**
- The content you see is **not random**—it is **carefully selected by AI to maximize engagement**, often

prioritizing **sensationalist and emotionally charged content.**

- **Echo chambers** reinforce **existing beliefs**, preventing independent thinking.

☐ **Example: How Social Media Influenced Elections**

- **2016 U.S. Election:** Russian bots used Facebook to spread **misinformation and political division.**

- **Myanmar Genocide (2016-2018):** Facebook's algorithm **amplified hate speech**, contributing to real-world violence.

☐ **Lesson:** If you don't control the **information you consume,** someone else controls **your thoughts.**

---

5. Education as a Tool of Control

Most people believe education exists to **empower individuals.** But in many cases, school systems are **designed to create obedient workers, not independent thinkers.**

☐ **How Schools Shape Perception**

☐ **Memorization Over Critical Thinking** – Schools **train obedience** rather than questioning.

☐ **History is Sanitized** – Textbooks often **ignore uncomfortable truths** (e.g., colonialism, corporate exploitation).

☐ **Civics & Economics are Downplayed** – Students **aren't taught how the system actually works**, preventing political and financial empowerment.

☐ **Example: Erasing Labor Rights & Worker Struggles**

- Schools rarely teach **how workers fought for the 8-hour workday, minimum wage, and labor laws.**

- As a result, younger generations are **less aware of their rights, making them easier to exploit.**

☐ **Lesson:** The education system often teaches **what benefits the ruling class, not what empowers individuals.**

6. How to Resist Perception Manipulation

✓ **Question Everything**

- Who owns the news you consume?
- Who benefits from the narratives being pushed?

✓ **Diversify Your Information Sources**

- Read **independent journalism, international news, and declassified documents.**
- Follow **historians, economists, and researchers—not just mainstream media.**

✓ **Build Media Literacy**

- Learn **how propaganda works** so you can recognize and resist it.
- Fact-check information before sharing it.

✓ **Strengthen Financial & Political Awareness**

- Understand **who funds politicians** and how **corporate money influences laws.**
- Support **policies and movements that reduce corporate and government overreach.**

Final Thought: You Are Not Powerless, But You Are Being Controlled

☐ **Governments and corporations do not control the world through force alone—they control it by shaping how people think.**

☐ If you believe what they want you to believe, you'll do what they want you to do.

☐ The first step to reclaiming power is recognizing when you are being manipulated.

The question isn't whether you're being influenced—it's whether you're willing to break free. ☐

CHAPTER 18: THE PSYCHOLOGICAL TACTICS USED TO MAKE PEOPLE FEEL POWERLESS

"A controlled mind is a defeated mind. The system does not need to use force if it can convince you that resistance is futile."

Governments, corporations, and other powerful institutions don't always need direct oppression to control people. Instead, they use psychological tactics to create a sense of helplessness, discouraging resistance, activism, and independent thought.

By making ordinary citizens feel powerless, the system ensures **compliance, obedience, and political inaction.** This chapter uncovers the most common **psychological tactics used to suppress individual empowerment** and how to break free from them.

1. Learned Helplessness: Making People Accept Their Fate

"Why try to change things if nothing will ever improve?"

One of the most effective psychological tactics used to suppress the ordinary citizen is **learned helplessness**—a state in which people **stop resisting oppression because they believe their actions won't make a difference.**

☐ **How It Works**

- When people experience **failure or oppression repeatedly**, they begin to believe **change is impossible.**
- Governments and corporations reinforce this by **creating the illusion that the system cannot be changed.**
- **Example:** In authoritarian regimes, after years of censorship and police brutality, many people **stop protesting altogether** because they believe resistance is futile.

☐ **Real-World Examples**

☐ **Voter Apathy:** Many citizens **stop voting** because they believe elections are rigged or that "nothing ever changes."

☐ **Economic Struggles:** Workers accept **low wages and exploitation** because they believe there are no better options.

☐ **Social Injustice:** Marginalized groups stop fighting for their rights because **oppression feels never-ending.**

☐ **Lesson:** The first step to reclaiming power is **rejecting the belief that resistance is useless.** Every movement in history started with **people who refused to give up.**

2. Divide & Conquer: Keeping the People Fighting Each Other

"As long as the people are divided, they will never rise against their true oppressors."

A **divided population is easier to control.** Governments and corporations **intentionally pit people against each other**—by race, class, religion, or political beliefs—so they don't unite against **the true sources of oppression.**

⬜ **How It Works**

⬜ **Encouraging Political & Racial Division** – Instead of fighting corrupt leaders, people fight each other.
⬜ **Fueling Class Resentment** – The poor blame the middle class, the middle class blames immigrants, but **no one blames the billionaires.**
⬜ **Distracting from Real Issues** – Governments create **"culture wars"** so people focus on social issues rather than economic exploitation.

⬜ **Real-World Examples**

⬜ **The U.S. Two-Party System:** Instead of challenging corporate rule, citizens are told their enemy is the "other political party."
⬜ **Colonial Strategy:** British and French colonizers **intentionally divided ethnic groups** so they would not unite against imperial rule.
⬜ **Workplace Divisions:** Corporations **pit workers against each other** (e.g., permanent employees vs. contract workers) to prevent unionizing.

⬜ **Lesson:** The system benefits when **the oppressed fight each other instead of uniting against oppression.** Recognize division tactics and refuse to be manipulated.

---

3. Fear-Based Control: Keeping People in a Permanent State of Anxiety

"A fearful population is an obedient population."

Governments and corporations **exploit fear** to keep people dependent, passive, and compliant. When people are scared—of crime, terrorism, pandemics, or financial collapse—they are **more likely to accept authoritarian control.**

⬜ **How It Works**

☐ **Fear of Uncertainty:** Economic crashes, pandemics, and wars create **a permanent crisis mentality.**

☐ **Fear of Dissent:** Activists are branded as **"radicals" or "terrorists"** to discourage participation.

☐ **Fear of Poverty:** People **accept low wages and bad jobs** because they fear unemployment.

☐ **Real-World Examples**

☐ **Post-9/11 Surveillance:** Governments expanded mass surveillance under the excuse of "fighting terrorism."

☐ **COVID-19 & Corporate Profits:** While ordinary people were scared for their health, billionaires **made record profits during the pandemic.**

☐ **Police Brutality & Protest Suppression:** Fear of violence **discourages people from joining protests.**

☐ **Lesson:** Fear is used **to make people accept oppression.** The solution is **courage, knowledge, and collective action.**

---

4. Overwhelming People with Information: The Paralysis of Choice

"If people are too overwhelmed, they won't act."

In the digital age, people are bombarded with **endless information**, making it difficult to **distinguish truth from propaganda** or decide where to focus their energy.

☐ **How It Works**

☐ **Information Overload:** News cycles move so fast that people **become numb to injustice.**

☐ **Conflicting Narratives:** Fake news and government propaganda create **confusion, making it harder to take action.**

☐ **Social Media Addiction:** Algorithms **keep people distracted** rather than organizing for real change.

☐ **Real-World Examples**

☐ **Climate Change Apathy:** People are **so overwhelmed by crisis after crisis** that many choose to ignore the issue.

☐ **Endless Political Scandals:** A new scandal **every week prevents real accountability.**

☐ **Misinformation on Social Media:** Conflicting narratives about the same event make people distrust all news sources.

☐ **Lesson:** Focus on **what matters most, take small but meaningful actions, and don't let distraction turn into inaction.**

---

5. Normalizing Oppression: Making Injustice Feel Inevitable

"If you normalize oppression, people will stop resisting it."

Over time, **unjust conditions become accepted as "just the way things are."** Governments and corporations work to **normalize inequality, corruption, and exploitation** so that people stop seeing them as problems to be fixed.

☐ **How It Works**

☐ **Making Poverty Seem Natural** – Instead of fixing economic inequality, people are told to "work harder."

☐ **Normalizing Surveillance** – People stop questioning government spying because they believe "everyone is being watched anyway."

☐ **Militarizing Police** – Over time, **seeing police in riot gear becomes normal,** reducing resistance to authoritarianism.

☐ **Real-World Examples**

☐ **Low Wages & Gig Economy:** Young people are told that **unstable jobs are the "new normal,"** instead of demanding fair wages.

☐ **Police Brutality:** After years of exposure, people **become desensitized** to state violence.

☐ **Mass Surveillance:** People **accept being watched at all times** because it's been normalized.

☐ **Lesson:** Just because oppression is common **does not mean it is inevitable.** If past generations fought for change, **so can we.**

---

6. Breaking Free: How to Regain Power

☐ **Recognize Manipulation:** Be aware of the psychological tactics used to keep you passive.

☐ **Educate Yourself & Others:** Read independent sources, study history, and understand power structures.

☐ **Reject Division:** Find common ground with others, even if you disagree on certain issues.

☐ **Turn Fear into Action:** Instead of being paralyzed by fear, **use it as motivation to organize and resist.**

☐ **Demand Change:** Challenge unfair systems through **protests, unions, petitions, and collective action.**

Final Thought: You Are Not Powerless

☐ **The system survives by making people feel helpless—but history proves that when ordinary citizens unite, they win.**

☐ **Every great revolution, every worker's strike, every civil rights movement started with people who refused to believe they were powerless.**

The question is not whether you are controlled—the question is, will you fight back? ☐

CHAPTER 19: STRATEGIES TO BREAK FREE FROM SYSTEMIC CONTROL

"The first step to breaking free is realizing that you are being controlled."

Governments, corporations, and media institutions use psychological, economic, and social tactics to maintain power over individuals. However, history has shown that ordinary citizens can reclaim their power through awareness, strategic action, and collective resistance.

This chapter explores **practical strategies** to **break free from systemic control**, regain autonomy, and **create meaningful change in society.**

---

1. Cultivate Independent Thinking: Break the Chains of Mental Conditioning

☐ *The system controls people by shaping their beliefs from an early age.*

☐ **How to Break Free from Indoctrination**

✓ **Question Everything:** Who benefits from the information you consume?

✓ **Expose Yourself to Different Perspectives:** Read diverse sources, including **independent media, history books, and alternative viewpoints.**

✓ **Recognize Manipulation Tactics:** Understand **fear-based propaganda, corporate influence, and political deception.**

☐ **Key Actions**

☐ **Diversify Your News Sources:** Follow **independent journalism, investigative reporters, and whistleblower accounts.**

☐ **Study History:** Learn **how past revolutions and social movements overcame oppression.**

☐ **Think Critically:** Always ask, **"Who profits from this narrative?"**

☐ **Lesson:** The first battle is **mental.** If you control your mind, **no system can truly control you.**

---

2. Achieve Economic Independence: Reduce Reliance on the System

☐ *Governments and corporations control individuals by keeping them financially dependent.*

☐ **How to Break Free from Financial Control**

✓ **Reduce Debt:** Debt is a tool of control. Pay off loans, avoid credit card traps, and live within your means.

✓ **Invest in Financial Literacy:** Learn about **investing, saving, and alternative economic models** (cooperatives, community banks, crypto, etc.).

✓ **Support Small & Ethical Businesses:** Avoid monopolies— spend your money in ways that support economic freedom.

☐ **Key Actions**

☐ **Create Multiple Income Streams:** Don't rely on a single employer—**freelancing, side businesses, and passive income** offer security.

◻ **Avoid Lifestyle Inflation:** Many people increase spending as they earn more, keeping themselves trapped in **consumerism.**

◻ **Shift to Decentralized Financial Systems:** Learn about **Bitcoin, community lending, and ethical investing.**

◻ **Lesson: The less you depend on corporations and government systems for survival, the more power you reclaim.**

---

3. Escape the Media Matrix: Control Your Own Information Flow

◻ *Mainstream media is designed to shape public perception and distract from real issues.*

◻ **How to Break Free from Media Manipulation**

✓ **Limit Exposure to Corporate News:** Diversify your sources—**follow independent journalists, whistleblowers, and alternative media.**

✓ **Understand Psychological Tactics:** Be aware of **fear-based news, distraction techniques, and emotional manipulation.**

✓ **Use Technology Wisely:** Social media algorithms are designed to **trap you in echo chambers—be intentional about what you consume.**

◻ **Key Actions**

◻ **Follow Investigative Journalists:** Support those who challenge the system rather than mainstream corporate media.

◻ **Fact-Check Everything:** Before sharing information, verify it with multiple reliable sources.

◻ **Avoid Doomscrolling:** The media profits from keeping people **fearful and anxious—limit consumption of negative news.**

◻ **Lesson:** If you **control your information intake,** you control your **mindset and decisions.**

---

4. Build Local & Global Networks: Strength in Numbers

❑ *The system thrives on isolation—real power comes from collective action.*

❑ **How to Break Free from Social Control**

✓ **Engage in Community Organizing:** Join **grassroots movements, unions, and activist groups** that align with your values.

✓ **Create Alternative Social Structures:** Build **community-based economies, education cooperatives, and decentralized networks.**

✓ **Leverage the Power of Online Activism:** While real-world action is crucial, **social media is a powerful tool for mobilization.**

❑ **Key Actions**

❑ **Participate in Local Politics:** Change starts at the local level—attend town hall meetings and vote in city elections.

❑ **Join or Start a Mutual Aid Network:** Help people in your community with **food, housing, legal support, and resources.**

❑ **Resist Divide-and-Conquer Tactics:** Find common ground with people across political and social differences.

❑ **Lesson: United communities can resist oppression better than isolated individuals.**

---

5. Take Back Political Power: Demand Systemic Change

❑ *Politicians serve corporate interests unless the people demand accountability.*

❑ **How to Break Free from Political Control**

✓ **Reject the Two-Party Illusion:** Many political systems offer only the **illusion of choice** while serving the same elite interests.

✓ **Push for Structural Reform:** Support changes that **reduce corporate influence, increase transparency, and strengthen direct democracy.**

✓ **Engage in Civic Resistance:** Protest, organize, and challenge unfair laws and policies.

☐ **Key Actions**

☐ **Vote Strategically:** Support candidates who actually challenge the system, not just the status quo.
☐ **Use Direct Action:** Protests, boycotts, and strikes have historically forced governments to listen.
☐ **Educate Others:** Help others understand **how the political system is structured to limit real change.**

☐ **Lesson:** If people **stop participating in a corrupt system**, it loses legitimacy. **Mass refusal is a powerful weapon.**

---

6. Control Your Own Narrative: Reclaim the Culture

☐ *The system controls people by defining what is "normal" and what is "radical."*

☐ **How to Break Free from Cultural Programming**

✓ **Reject Consumerism:** You don't need **corporate brands, luxury goods, or material possessions** to define your worth.
✓ **Promote Alternative Ideas:** Support **independent artists, activists, and thinkers** who challenge the system.
✓ **Be the Media:** Create content that **educates, inspires, and mobilizes.**

☐ **Key Actions**

☐ **Support Ethical Media & Art:** Shift support to creators who **challenge mainstream narratives.**
☐ **Create Your Own Content:** If you have a voice, use it—**write, make videos, organize discussions.**
☐ **Reject Elitist Definitions of Success:** Success isn't about wealth—it's about **freedom, purpose, and impact.**

☐ **Lesson:** The system shapes culture to benefit the elite. **Reclaim culture to benefit the people.**

---

7. Develop Self-Sufficiency: Reduce Dependence on the System

The more independent you are, the less control the system has over you.

How to Break Free from Total Dependence

✓ **Grow Your Own Food:** Even small-scale gardening **reduces reliance on industrial agriculture.**

✓ **Develop Practical Skills:** Learn **basic survival skills, first aid, and DIY repair.**

✓ **Disconnect from Corporate Systems:** Use **alternative energy, local food sources, and decentralized digital networks.**

Key Actions

Reduce Energy Dependence: Explore **solar, wind, and off-grid living solutions.**

Master Basic Survival Skills: Learn how to **cook, fix things, and grow food.**

Share Skills & Knowledge: Teach others how to **become more independent.**

Lesson: The less you rely on the system, **the more control you have over your life.**

Final Thought: Freedom is a Choice

The system wants you to believe you are powerless. But history shows that ordinary people, when united and aware, can overthrow even the most oppressive regimes.

You do not have to accept the conditions imposed on you. You can resist, adapt, and create a new way of living.

The first step to breaking free is deciding that you will no longer be controlled.

The question isn't whether you can break free—the question is, are you willing to take the first step?

CHAPTER 20: MISINFORMATION & THE BATTLE FOR TRUTH

"In a world where deception is power, truth becomes the ultimate weapon."

Misinformation is one of the most powerful tools used to control society. Governments, corporations, and media outlets deliberately spread false or misleading information to shape public opinion, suppress dissent, and maintain control.

In the digital age, **the battle for truth has become more critical than ever.** With millions of people consuming news through social media and online platforms, **disinformation campaigns can spread faster than facts.** This chapter explores how misinformation is used as a weapon, who benefits from it, and how ordinary citizens can fight back.

1. What is Misinformation and Why is it So Dangerous?

Misinformation refers to false or misleading information spread intentionally or unintentionally.

There are two main types:

1 **Misinformation** – False or misleading information shared by mistake.

2 **Disinformation** – False information deliberately created to deceive people.

Why is Misinformation So Effective?

- **It Exploits Emotions** – People are more likely to believe and share information that triggers fear, anger, or hope.

- **It Spreads Faster Than the Truth** – False news spreads **six times faster** than true news on social media.

- **It Confirms Biases** – People tend to believe information that supports their existing beliefs, even if it's false.

Lesson: The most dangerous lies are the ones people **want to believe.**

---

2. Who Benefits from Misinformation?

Misinformation is never random—it always serves a purpose.

Governments Use Misinformation to Stay in Power

- **Dictatorships use censorship & propaganda** to rewrite history and suppress dissent.

- **Democratic governments use spin and controlled narratives** to justify wars, surveillance, and economic policies.

- **Example:** In 2003, U.S. media repeatedly reported that Iraq had "weapons of mass destruction" (WMDs), leading to war. **The weapons never existed.**

Corporations Use Misinformation for Profit

- **Big Pharma manipulates medical studies** to promote

expensive drugs over cheaper alternatives.

- **Food & beverage companies fund misleading research** to hide the dangers of sugar, processed food, and artificial chemicals.

- **Example:** The tobacco industry spent decades **spreading fake science** to deny the health risks of smoking.

◻ **Political & Ideological Groups Use Misinformation to Divide Society**

- **False narratives about race, gender, and class** are spread to divide people and prevent unity.

- **Fear-based propaganda** creates enemies and distractions to shift focus from real issues.

- **Example:** During elections, **false stories about candidates** are spread to manipulate public perception.

◻ **Lesson:** If a false narrative is being aggressively pushed, **ask yourself who benefits from it.**

---

3. How Social Media Algorithms Amplify Misinformation

◻ *Social media doesn't just spread misinformation—it supercharges it.*

◻ **The Algorithm Problem**

- Platforms like **Facebook, Twitter, and YouTube prioritize engagement, not truth.**

- **Sensational headlines and conspiracy theories** get more clicks and shares than factual reporting.

- **Echo chambers reinforce misinformation**, making people more resistant to truth.

◻ **Example: The Facebook Scandal**

- In 2016, **Russian bots used Facebook to spread fake**

news during the U.S. presidential election.

- The platform's algorithm **amplified misinformation, reaching millions of people.**
- Facebook later admitted it **prioritized profits over preventing disinformation.**

☐ **Lesson: Social media is designed to keep people engaged—not informed.**

---

4. How Governments & Corporations Use Misinformation to Suppress Truth

☐ *When truth threatens power, those in control will attack it.*

☐ **Silencing Whistleblowers & Journalists**

- **Truth-tellers are often punished for exposing corruption and injustice.**
- **Example:**
  - **Julian Assange (WikiLeaks)** exposed war crimes and was imprisoned.
  - **Edward Snowden** revealed mass government surveillance and had to flee his country.
  - **Journalists investigating corporate corruption** often face lawsuits, threats, or murder.

☐ **Rewriting History & Distorting Facts**

- Governments **rewrite history books** to hide their crimes and glorify their actions.
- Corporations **control academic research** to promote their agendas.
- **Example:** U.S. history textbooks often **downplay slavery and colonialism** to create a more favorable national image.

☐ **Lesson: History is written by the victors, but the truth is told by those who dare to expose them.**

5. How to Recognize & Defend Against Misinformation

☐ The best way to fight misinformation is through critical thinking and independent research.

☐ How to Spot Misinformation

✓ **Check the Source:** Who published the information? Is it a respected, independent source?

✓ **Look for Evidence:** Does the article cite facts, or is it just emotional claims?

✓ **Verify with Multiple Sources:** If only one news outlet is reporting something, be skeptical.

✓ **Beware of Clickbait & Sensational Headlines:** If a headline seems too outrageous, it's probably misleading.

✓ **Check for Bias:** Is the story designed to push a political or corporate agenda?

☐ Where to Find Reliable Information

☐ **Independent journalism** – Investigative outlets like ProPublica, The Intercept, and Consortium News.

☐ **Fact-checking sites** – Snopes, FactCheck.org, and Media Bias/Fact Check.

☐ **Academic sources & declassified documents** – University studies and government transparency reports.

☐ Lesson: Truth takes effort—lies spread effortlessly.

6. The Future of Misinformation: AI, Deepfakes & Digital Deception

☐ As technology evolves, misinformation is becoming harder to detect.

☐ The Rise of AI-Generated Fake News

- **AI can now create fake news articles, fake videos, and even fake social media profiles.**
- **Deepfake technology can manipulate videos**, making

it appear that politicians or celebrities said things they never did.

Example: The Deepfake Problem

- In 2021, a deepfake video of **Ukrainian President Volodymyr Zelensky "surrendering" to Russia** was released online. It was fake—but many believed it.

How to Prepare for a Future of Digital Deception

✓ **Learn Digital Literacy:** Understand how deepfakes and AI-generated content work.

✓ **Support Decentralized & Transparent Media:** Move away from corporate-controlled platforms.

✓ **Advocate for Ethical AI Use:** Push for regulations on deepfake technology and AI-generated propaganda.

Lesson: Future misinformation will be harder to detect—but awareness is our best defense.

---

7. How Ordinary People Can Win the Battle for Truth

Key Actions to Take

✓ **Be a Truth-Seeker:** Always question and verify information.

✓ **Educate Others:** Teach friends and family how to identify misinformation.

✓ **Support Independent Journalists & Whistleblowers:** Follow those who expose corruption.

✓ **Resist Emotional Manipulation:** If a story makes you **angry, fearful, or outraged, pause and fact-check before reacting.**

✓ **Spread Verified Truths:** Correct misinformation when you see it.

Lesson: The battle for truth is fought one person at a time. If you refuse to be manipulated, you become part of the solution.

Final Thought: Truth is Power

Misinformation is the most effective weapon of control—but truth is the greatest tool of resistance.

☐ Every dictatorship, corrupt government, and exploitative corporation relies on lies to survive. The moment people stop believing their lies, they lose their power.

☐ The system fears informed, critical-thinking citizens more than anything. Be one of them.

The question is not whether misinformation exists—the question is, will you be its victim or its opponent? ☐

CHAPTER 21: THE RISE OF FAKE NEWS AND ITS EFFECT ON PUBLIC OPINION

"A lie can travel halfway around the world while the truth is still putting on its shoes." — Mark Twain

In the digital age, fake news has become a weapon of mass deception, influencing elections, shaping public opinion, and creating societal division. While misinformation has always existed, the internet and social media have supercharged its spread, making it harder to distinguish truth from lies.

This chapter explores **how fake news emerged, how it manipulates public perception, and how ordinary citizens can defend themselves against it.**

---

1. What is Fake News?

 Fake news refers to false or misleading information presented as legitimate journalism to deceive or manipulate people.

▢ Types of Fake News

▢ Outright Fabrications – Completely false stories made up to mislead (e.g., "The Pope Endorses Trump").
▢ Manipulated Headlines – Articles that twist facts or exaggerate claims for emotional reactions.
▢ Satirical News Taken Seriously – Some people mistake humor-based content (e.g., The Onion) as factual news.
▢ Misused Data & Misleading Reports – Statistics and studies taken out of context to support an agenda.
▢ Deepfakes & Altered Media – AI-generated images, videos, and audio designed to create false realities.

▢ Lesson: Fake news is not just about lies—it's about controlling how people perceive reality.

---

2. How Fake News Became a Global Crisis

▢ The Digital Revolution Changed How People Consume News

- In the past, newspapers, radio, and TV controlled information flow.
- Today, **anyone can create and share "news" online—without fact-checking.**
- Social media platforms **prioritize engagement over accuracy**, amplifying **outrage and sensationalism.**

▢ The Business of Fake News

- Fake news generates **high engagement, leading to massive ad revenue.**
- **Clickbait headlines** manipulate emotions, making people more likely to share them.
- **Example:** Fake news sites made **millions of dollars during the 2016 U.S. election** by publishing fabricated political stories.

▢ The Role of Social Media Algorithms

- Facebook, Twitter, and YouTube promote content

based on engagement, not truth.

- Misinformation spreads six times faster than real news.
- **Example:** False stories about COVID-19 vaccines spread faster than verified medical information.

☐ **Lesson:** Fake news is not just **an accident—it is a business model built on manipulation and profit.**

---

3. How Fake News Manipulates Public Opinion

☐ **Psychological Triggers Used in Fake News**

☐ **Fear & Panic:** Fake news often creates crises that don't exist.

☐ **Confirmation Bias:** People believe stories that support their existing opinions.

☐ **Tribalism:** Fake news divides people into **"us vs. them"** mentalities.

☐ **Real-World Examples of Fake News Impacting Society**

☐ **The 2016 U.S. Election**

- False reports claimed **Hillary Clinton was running a child trafficking ring** out of a pizza shop (Pizzagate).
- A man with a gun stormed the restaurant, believing he was saving children from abuse.

☐ **The COVID-19 Pandemic**

- False claims about **microchips in vaccines** led to vaccine hesitancy.
- Fake "cures" like **drinking bleach** resulted in real-world harm.

☐ **Anti-Immigrant & Racial Fake News**

- Fabricated stories about **migrants committing crimes** have fueled xenophobia.
- Fake statistics have been used to justify **harsh immigration policies.**

☐ **Lesson:** Fake news has real-world consequences, influencing elections, public health, and social policies.

---

4. How Governments & Corporations Use Fake News to Their Advantage

☐ *Fake news is often weaponized by those in power to control narratives and suppress opposition.*

☐ How Governments Use Fake News

☐ **Propaganda & Censorship:** Authoritarian regimes flood social media with **state-approved lies** while censoring the truth.

☐ **Election Manipulation:** Foreign and domestic actors use fake news to **influence voter behavior** (e.g., Russian interference in U.S. elections).

☐ **Justifying War & Oppression:** Governments fabricate crises to **justify military actions and emergency laws** (e.g., Iraq's "Weapons of Mass Destruction" lie).

☐ How Corporations Benefit from Fake News

☐ **False Advertising & Health Misinformation:** Big Pharma, food companies, and tobacco industries have spread **fake science** to protect profits.

☐ **Astroturfing:** Companies create **fake grassroots movements** to push corporate agendas (e.g., fossil fuel companies funding climate change denial).

☐ **Lesson:** Fake news isn't just an accident—it is **a tool used by those in power to shape reality in their favor.**

---

5. How to Recognize and Resist Fake News

☐ *To fight fake news, people must learn critical thinking skills and media literacy.*

☐ How to Spot Fake News

✓ **Check the Source:** Is it from a credible outlet, or a random website?

✓ **Verify with Multiple Sources:** If only one place is reporting a major story, be skeptical.

✓ **Look for Emotional Manipulation:** If a story makes you **extremely angry or fearful**, it might be fake.

✓ **Check for Expert Opinions:** Is the story supported by **qualified professionals, scientists, or historians?**

✓ **Use Fact-Checking Websites:** Snopes, FactCheck.org, and PolitiFact can debunk many false claims.

Digital Tools to Fight Fake News

 Google Reverse Image Search – Helps detect **fake or manipulated images.**

 NewsGuard Browser Extension – Rates news sites for credibility.

 Deepfake Detection Tools – AI-powered apps that identify altered videos.

 Lesson: The best defense against fake news is an informed, skeptical mind.

---

6. The Future of Fake News: Deepfakes & AI Manipulation

Fake news is evolving, making it harder to detect lies from reality.

The Rise of Deepfake Technology

- AI can **create realistic videos of people saying things they never said.**

- Politicians, celebrities, and journalists **can be impersonated** to spread misinformation.

- **Example:** In 2022, a deepfake video showed Ukrainian President Zelensky telling his troops to surrender—**it was fake, but some believed it.**

AI-Generated Fake News

- AI can now write **entire fake articles**, making fact-checking more difficult.

- Chatbots can be programmed to **spread propaganda at massive scales.**

How to Prepare for the Next Wave of Fake News

✓ **Learn About Deepfake Detection Tools.**
✓ **Advocate for Digital Literacy Education in Schools.**
✓ **Support Transparency Laws for AI-Generated Content.**

☐ **Lesson:** The next phase of fake news will be **harder to detect— but awareness is our greatest weapon.**

---

7. How Ordinary People Can Fight Back Against Fake News

☐ Key Actions to Take

✓ **Educate Yourself & Others** – Teach media literacy skills in your community.
✓ **Verify Before Sharing** – Never spread unverified information, even if it aligns with your beliefs.
✓ **Support Ethical Journalism** – Follow independent media and investigative journalists.
✓ **Call Out Misinformation** – Politely challenge fake news when you see it online.
✓ **Advocate for Stronger Tech Regulations** – Push for transparency in algorithms and AI-generated content.

☐ **Lesson: Truth wins when individuals take responsibility for what they believe, share, and support.**

Final Thought: Truth is a Revolutionary Act

☐ **Fake news is not just a nuisance—it is a tool of control.**
☐ **It is used to divide, manipulate, and distract people from real issues.**
☐ **But if enough people choose truth over deception, lies lose their power.**

The question is not whether fake news exists—the question is, will you let it control what you believe? ☐

CHAPTER 22:
TOOLS TO IDENTIFY AND COMBAT MISINFORMATION

"In an era of deception, truth-seeking is a revolutionary act."

Misinformation is one of the biggest threats to democracy, public health, and social stability. To fight back, individuals must equip themselves with the right tools and strategies to detect and combat false narratives. This chapter provides **practical tools and techniques** to help ordinary citizens identify fake news, fact-check suspicious claims, and become more resilient against manipulation.

1. The Basics of Identifying Misinformation

Before diving into specific tools, it's important to recognize **the common signs of misinformation.**

☐ **Five Red Flags of Misinformation**

 Emotional Manipulation – Does the content trigger **anger, fear, or outrage** without solid evidence?

 Lack of Sources or Anonymous Claims – Does the article fail to cite **credible experts or sources**?

 Clickbait Headlines – Is the title **sensationalized or exaggerated** to grab attention?

 One-Sided or Extreme Bias – Does the content **attack a particular group or political ideology** without balanced reporting?

 Mismatched Images & Videos – Does the image or video match the context of the story? (Often, old images are reused to create false narratives.)

 Lesson: Misinformation often relies on emotions rather than facts. Always pause and verify before believing or sharing.

2. Fact-Checking Websites

These platforms specialize in **verifying news, debunking hoaxes, and exposing propaganda.**

 Global Fact-Checking Sites

 Snopes (snopes.com) – One of the most trusted sites for debunking viral hoaxes and misinformation.

 FactCheck.org (factcheck.org) – A nonpartisan organization that investigates political claims.

 PolitiFact (politifact.com) – Specializes in checking statements made by politicians and public figures.

 Reuters Fact Check (reuters.com/fact-check) – A major international news agency fact-checking misinformation.

 BBC Reality Check (bbc.com/realitycheck) – Investigates misleading stories and viral misinformation.

 Lesson: If a claim sounds suspicious, **cross-check it with at least one of these sites.**

3. Tools for Verifying Images & Videos

Misinformation often spreads **through altered images and**

deepfake videos. Use these tools to verify authenticity.

☐ Reverse Image Search

☐ **Google Reverse Image Search** (images.google.com) – Upload an image to see where it originally appeared.

☐ **TinEye** (tineye.com) – Detects altered images and identifies their source.

☐ Deepfake & Video Verification Tools

☐ **InVID & WeVerify** (invid-project.eu) – Analyzes videos to detect deepfakes and manipulated footage.

☐ **Microsoft Video Authenticator** – A tool designed to detect deepfake videos by analyzing digital artifacts.

☐ **Lesson: If an image or video seems too shocking or outrageous, verify its authenticity before believing it.**

---

4. Browser Extensions for Fake News Detection

These tools help you evaluate the credibility of websites and detect misinformation as you browse the internet.

☐ Browser Add-ons for Fact-Checking & Bias Detection

☐ **NewsGuard** (newsguardtech.com) – Rates the credibility of news websites and flags unreliable sources.

☐ **Fakey** (fakey.iuni.iu.edu) – Trains users to recognize fake news while browsing.

☐ **B.S. Detector** – Flags known sources of fake news and unreliable reporting.

☐ **Lesson: Installing a browser extension can help you avoid misinformation before you even click on a link.**

---

5. Social Media Verification Tools

Since social media is **the main battleground for misinformation**, these tools can help you verify posts before sharing.

☐ Twitter & Facebook Fact-Checking

◻ **Twitter's Birdwatch** (twitter.com/i/birdwatch) – Allows users to flag misleading tweets and add context.

◻ **Facebook Fact-Checking Labels** – Meta partners with independent fact-checkers to flag false information.

◻ **Tools to Analyze Social Media Accounts**

◻ **Bot Sentinel** (botsentinel.com) – Detects bot accounts spreading misinformation on Twitter.

◻ **Hoaxy** (hoaxy.iuni.iu.edu) – Tracks how fake news spreads on social media.

◻ **Lesson: Before sharing a post, check if it's flagged by fact-checkers or coming from a suspicious account.**

---

6. Strategies to Avoid Falling for Misinformation

◻ **How to Strengthen Your Own Fact-Checking Skills**

✓ **Pause Before Sharing:** Don't spread information unless you're sure it's true.

✓ **Look for the Original Source:** Don't rely on screenshots or secondhand claims—find the primary source.

✓ **Compare Multiple News Outlets:** If only one side of the political spectrum is reporting a story, be skeptical.

✓ **Check Dates & Context:** Old news is sometimes reshared to create false narratives.

✓ **Be Skeptical of Viral Posts:** Just because something is trending doesn't mean it's true.

◻ **How to Talk to Someone Who Believes Fake News**

◻ **Stay Calm:** Confronting someone aggressively makes them defensive.

◻ **Ask Questions:** Encourage them to think critically—"Where did you hear that?"

◻ **Provide Evidence:** Share links to fact-checking websites and reputable sources.

◻ **Find Common Ground:** Instead of arguing, focus on shared values and the importance of truth.

☐ **Lesson: Fighting misinformation is not just about proving someone wrong—it's about helping them see the truth.**

---

7. How Governments & Tech Companies Should Combat Fake News

☐ *While individuals can fight misinformation, large-scale action is needed from governments and tech companies.*

☐ **Policy Solutions**

✓ **Regulate Social Media Algorithms:** Platforms should **prioritize factual content** over viral misinformation.
✓ **Increase Transparency:** Political ads and sponsored content should be clearly labeled.
✓ **Strengthen Digital Literacy in Schools:** Critical thinking and media literacy should be **mandatory subjects.**

☐ **What Tech Companies Must Do**

✓ **Remove Fake Accounts & Bots:** AI-driven misinformation campaigns should be shut down.
✓ **Expand Fact-Checking Partnerships:** More collaborations with **independent fact-checkers.**
✓ **Promote Reliable Sources:** News from **verified organizations should rank higher** than conspiracy sites.

☐ **Lesson:** The fight against misinformation requires **policy change, tech accountability, and public awareness.**

Final Thought: Truth is a Responsibility

☐ **Misinformation thrives when people stop questioning. Truth wins when individuals commit to critical thinking.**
☐ **By using the right tools and strategies, you can become a guardian of truth in an age of deception.**
☐ **Misinformation is a weapon—make sure you're not its victim.**

The question isn't whether fake news exists—the question is, will you be fooled by it? ☐

CHAPTER 23: THE ROLE OF EDUCATION IN STRENGTHENING CIVIC AWARENESS

"An educated mind is the most powerful weapon against oppression."

E ducation is not just about acquiring knowledge—it is a tool for empowerment, critical thinking, and civic engagement. Societies that invest in civic education create informed, active citizens who can challenge corruption, demand accountability, and drive meaningful change.

However, many education systems fail to teach people how to be **engaged citizens, question authority, or understand their rights.** This chapter explores **how education strengthens civic awareness, how it is often manipulated by those in power, and what can be done to improve it.**

1. What is Civic Awareness, and Why Does It Matter?

☐ *Civic awareness refers to an individual's understanding of their rights, responsibilities, and role in society.*

Key Elements of Civic Awareness

Understanding of Laws & Rights – Knowing legal protections and obligations.

Political Literacy – Understanding how governments work and how policies are made.

Media Literacy – Being able to distinguish **truth from misinformation.**

Social Responsibility – Recognizing the importance of **community service and activism.**

Why Civic Awareness is Important

- **Prevents authoritarianism** – Educated citizens are less likely to accept government overreach.

- **Strengthens democracy** – Informed voters make better decisions.

- **Fights corruption** – Citizens who know their rights are more likely to hold leaders accountable.

- **Encourages activism** – Awareness leads to action in social justice movements.

Lesson: The stronger the civic awareness in a society, the more resistant it is to manipulation and control.

---

2. The Role of Schools in Teaching Civic Engagement

A strong education system should not just teach math and science —it should teach people how to be active citizens.

How Schools Can Build Civic Awareness

✓ **Teach Critical Thinking** – Encourage students to **question authority and analyze information.**

✓ **Teach History Accurately** – Provide **unbiased accounts of civil rights movements, revolutions, and government failures.**

✓ **Include Political Education** – Explain **how laws are passed, how voting works, and how to engage in activism.**

✓ **Encourage Debate & Discussion** – Allow students to **analyze policies and express their opinions freely.**

☐ **Examples of Effective Civic Education**

☐ **Finland** – Students learn **critical thinking, media literacy, and civic responsibility.**
☐ **Denmark** – Schools prioritize **open debates on politics and governance.**
☐ **Taiwan** – Integrates **digital literacy programs** to combat misinformation.

☐ **Lesson:** The best education systems prepare students **not just for jobs, but for active participation in democracy.**

---

3. How Governments Manipulate Education to Suppress Civic Awareness

☐ *When education is controlled by those in power, it can be used as a tool for manipulation rather than empowerment.*

☐ **Tactics Used to Control Education**

☐ **Censoring History** – Hiding past injustices to protect the government's image.
☐ **Discouraging Critical Thinking** – Teaching students to memorize facts rather than analyze issues.
☐ **Banning Political Discussions in Schools** – Preventing young people from engaging in activism.
☐ **Underfunding Public Education** – Keeping citizens ignorant to reduce resistance.

☐ **Examples of Educational Manipulation**

☐ **U.S. (Texas & Florida)** – Attempts to **rewrite history books to downplay slavery and racism.**
☐ **China** – Government censors **Tiananmen Square Massacre** from history lessons.
☐ **Russia** – Schools promote **pro-government propaganda while suppressing independent thought.**

☐ **Lesson: If education is controlled by the government, it can**

be used to shape obedience rather than independent thinking.

4. The Power of Media Literacy in Civic Education

⬚ *In the digital age, education must include media literacy to protect against misinformation and propaganda.*

⬚ **Why Media Literacy is Essential**

- **Prevents fake news from influencing elections.**
- **Teaches people to fact-check political claims.**
- **Encourages responsible social media usage.**

⬚ **How Schools Can Teach Media Literacy**

✓ **Train Students to Recognize Bias** – Teach how to identify **misleading headlines and biased reporting.**

✓ **Fact-Checking Exercises** – Encourage students to **verify news sources.**

✓ **Teach How Social Media Algorithms Work** – Explain how **platforms prioritize engagement over truth.**

✓ **Expose Government & Corporate Manipulation** – Discuss real-world examples of **propaganda and digital disinformation.**

⬚ **Lesson:** In the modern world, **media literacy is just as important as reading and writing.**

5. How Grassroots Movements Can Strengthen Civic Education

⬚ *When schools fail to teach civic engagement, grassroots organizations step in.*

⬚ **The Role of Activist Groups in Education**

⬚ **Workshops on Voting Rights & Political Systems.**
⬚ **Community-Led History & Social Justice Discussions.**
⬚ **Independent Media Projects to Spread Awareness.**
⬚ **Online Courses on Activism & Citizen Rights.**

⬚ **Examples of Grassroots Civic Education Initiatives**

⬚ **Black Lives Matter (BLM)** – Educates communities on **racial** injustice and legal rights.

◻ **Fridays for Future** – Teaches young people about **climate activism.**

◻ **The Sunrise Movement** – Focuses on **youth-led environmental and policy education.**

◻ **Lesson: Even when governments try to suppress education, people can take learning into their own hands.**

---

6. How to Strengthen Civic Awareness in Society

◻ **Key Actions for Individuals**

✓ **Educate Yourself on Political & Social Issues** – Read books, watch documentaries, and follow independent news.

✓ **Engage in Community Discussions** – Attend town halls, local meetings, and civic education programs.

✓ **Teach the Next Generation** – Talk to young people about history, politics, and activism.

✓ **Use Social Media to Spread Awareness** – Share verified facts and educate others on misinformation.

◻ **Key Actions for Governments & Schools**

✓ **Introduce Mandatory Civic Education** – Teach governance, law, and activism in schools.

✓ **Ensure Unbiased History Education** – Include civil rights movements and struggles against oppression.

✓ **Invest in Media Literacy Programs** – Teach how to analyze information critically.

✓ **Promote Youth Participation in Politics** – Lower voting ages, create student government programs, and encourage civic engagement.

◻ **Lesson:** Civic education must be a **lifelong commitment, not just a school subject.**

Final Thought: Knowledge is Power—Use It Wisely

◻ **A well-educated society is harder to manipulate, harder to** suppress, and harder to control.

☐ When citizens understand their rights, their government, and the power they hold, they become the greatest threat to oppression.

☐ The system wants an uninformed, passive population—education is the key to resistance.

The question is not whether civic awareness is important—the question is, will you take responsibility for strengthening it? ☐

CHAPTER 24: ECONOMIC INEQUALITY & THE STRUGGLE FOR FINANCIAL POWER

"The greatest tool of control is not chains or prisons—it is economic dependence."

E conomic inequality is one of the most powerful forces shaping modern society. The gap between the rich and the poor has widened dramatically, making it harder for ordinary citizens to gain financial stability, own property, or escape cycles of debt.

While billionaires and multinational corporations **accumulate extreme wealth, the majority of people struggle with stagnant wages, rising costs, and financial insecurity.** This chapter explores **how economic inequality is maintained, how it affects political power, and what can be done to fight back.**

1. The Growing Wealth Gap: How the System is Rigged for the Rich

The top 1% of the world's population controls more wealth than the bottom 99% combined.

The Reality of Wealth Inequality

CEOs earn 300-500 times more than their workers.
The average worker's wages have stagnated, while corporate profits soar.
The rich use tax loopholes to avoid paying their fair share, while the poor bear the tax burden.

The System is Designed to Keep the Wealthy on Top

Corporate Bailouts: Governments give billions in financial aid to corporations while refusing to cancel student debt.
Stock Market Manipulation: The wealthy benefit from insider trading and financial loopholes while ordinary investors struggle.
Real Estate Hoarding: Investors buy up housing, driving up rent and making home ownership impossible for young people.

Lesson: The economy is not broken—it is **built this way to benefit those already at the top.**

---

2. The Role of Governments in Maintaining Economic Inequality

Governments claim to serve the people, but their policies often favor corporations and the wealthy elite.

How Governments Protect the Rich

Low Taxes for the Wealthy: Billionaires pay lower tax rates than middle-class workers.
Deregulation of Corporations: Governments remove restrictions that allow big businesses to exploit workers and consumers.
Lack of Strong Labor Laws: Workers have fewer protections, allowing corporations to pay low wages and fire employees

easily.

☐ How Political Corruption Worsens Inequality

☐ **Lobbying & Corporate Donations:** The rich influence laws to protect their wealth.

☐ **Weak Antitrust Enforcement:** Governments allow monopolies to crush competition.

☐ **Cutting Public Services:** Education, healthcare, and social welfare programs are underfunded, forcing the poor to struggle more.

☐ **Lesson:** The political system is deeply tied to economic inequality—**real change requires breaking corporate control over government.**

---

3. The Impact of Economic Inequality on Ordinary Citizens

☐ *Financial struggles don't just affect individuals—they shape the entire society.*

☐ Effects of Economic Inequality

☐ **Rising Cost of Living** – Inflation increases, but wages stay the same.

☐ **Lack of Affordable Healthcare** – Many people avoid medical treatment due to high costs.

☐ **Educational Barriers** – The best schools and universities are out of reach for lower-income students.

☐ **Job Insecurity** – Workers fear losing their jobs due to outsourcing, automation, and corporate downsizing.

☐ **Mental Health Crisis** – Financial stress leads to anxiety, depression, and hopelessness.

☐ **Lesson:** Economic inequality is not just about money—it affects **health, education, and overall quality of life.**

---

4. How Debt is Used to Control the Population

☐ *Debt is the modern form of slavery—keeping people trapped in endless cycles of repayment.*

The Debt Trap

Student Loans: Young people start their lives in debt, limiting financial freedom.

Credit Cards & Payday Loans: High-interest rates keep people permanently indebted.

Mortgage & Rent Inflation: Homeownership is out of reach for most, forcing lifelong renting.

How the Rich Profit from Debt

- Banks and lenders **intentionally create loan systems** that are nearly impossible to escape.
- **Billionaires use debt to grow richer**, while the poor use debt just to survive.
- Governments **bail out banks** but refuse to help ordinary people struggling with debt.

Lesson: The financial system is designed to keep people **trapped in debt, not to help them build wealth.**

---

5. The Power of Collective Economic Action

Ordinary citizens can fight back against economic inequality by reclaiming financial power.

Strategies to Break Free from Economic Control

✓ **Support Labor Unions:** Higher wages and better working conditions come from collective bargaining.

✓ **Practice Ethical Spending:** Support small businesses instead of multinational corporations.

✓ **Invest in Financial Education:** Learn about savings, investments, and alternative economic models.

✓ **Push for Economic Policy Changes:** Demand higher taxes on the rich, universal healthcare, and free education.

Examples of Successful Economic Resistance

Worker Strikes – Employees at Amazon, Starbucks, and McDonald's have demanded better wages.

◻ **Boycotts Against Unethical Companies** – Consumer pressure has forced companies to change exploitative practices.

◻ **Alternative Economic Models** – Community-owned businesses and co-operatives offer fairer economic systems.

◻ **Lesson:** Economic power is not just about money—it is about **control, influence, and collective action.**

---

6. Alternative Economic Systems: Breaking Away from Capitalist Exploitation

◻ *The current economic system benefits the few at the expense of the many—but alternative models exist.*

◻ **Alternative Economic Models**

◻ **Worker Cooperatives:** Businesses owned by employees rather than corporations.

◻ **Universal Basic Income (UBI):** Guaranteed financial support for all citizens.

◻ **Participatory Economics:** Economic decisions are made collectively rather than by elites.

◻ **Public Banking:** Community-owned financial systems instead of corporate banks.

◻ **Lesson:** The economy is not fixed—**it can be changed to work for the people rather than just for corporations.**

---

7. How Individuals Can Reclaim Financial Power

◻ *Economic freedom requires strategic action, financial literacy, and collective effort.*

◻ **Steps to Take for Financial Independence**

✓ **Minimize Debt:** Pay off high-interest loans and avoid unnecessary credit.

✓ **Invest in Assets, Not Liabilities:** Focus on savings, property, and sustainable investments.

✓ **Support Fair Economic Policies:** Advocate for progressive taxation and corporate accountability.

✓ **Join Economic Activism Movements:** Work with groups fighting for higher wages, better labor rights, and financial reform.

☐ **The Power of Economic Independence**

☐ **The less dependent you are on corporations and the government, the more freedom you have.**
☐ **Learning how money works gives you power over your own future.**

☐ **Economic security allows you to focus on activism, creativity, and meaningful contributions to society.**

☐ **Lesson:** Taking control of your finances **is not just about personal success—it is about fighting economic oppression.**

Final Thought: Money is Power—Who Controls It?

☐ **Economic inequality is not an accident—it is designed to benefit the elite at the expense of the majority.**
☐ **Financial control is one of the greatest tools of oppression— but knowledge, collective action, and financial independence can break the cycle.**
☐ **The system thrives when ordinary people remain in financial struggle—will you choose to fight back?**

The question is not whether economic inequality exists—the question is, what will you do about it? ☐

CHAPTER 25: HOW THE FINANCIAL SYSTEM IS DESIGNED TO BENEFIT THE ELITE

"The financial system is not broken. It works exactly as intended—to keep the rich rich and the poor struggling."

The modern financial system is not designed for fairness—it is built to concentrate wealth at the top while keeping the majority financially dependent. From banking policies to stock markets, taxation, and corporate monopolies, every part of the system is structured to ensure the rich get richer while the working class remains trapped in economic struggle.

This chapter exposes the mechanisms that allow **the elite to accumulate extreme wealth while ordinary people fight for survival.**

1. The Wealth Trap: Why the Rich Keep Getting Richer

☐ *If you want to understand economic inequality, you have to* understand how wealth multiplies for the rich while disappearing for the poor.

☐ The Secret Formula: Passive Income vs. Wage Labor

☐ **The wealthy make money without working.** They own businesses, stocks, and real estate that generate income **even while they sleep.**

☐ **The poor and middle class trade time for money.** They depend on salaries, meaning they must keep working just to survive.

☐ **Example:** A billionaire's wealth **grows automatically** through stock market investments, while a worker's paycheck disappears on rent and bills.

☐ **Lesson:** The financial system rewards **ownership, not labor.** If you don't own assets, you stay trapped in the cycle.

---

2. The Banking System: How It Keeps the Poor in Debt

☐ *Banks are not designed to help people—they are designed to profit off them.*

☐ How Banks Exploit Ordinary Citizens

☐ **High-Interest Loans for the Poor, Low-Interest Loans for the Rich:**

- The poor are given **high-interest credit cards, student loans, and payday loans** that keep them in debt.
- The wealthy get **low-interest business loans and mortgages,** allowing them to build wealth.

☐ **Fractional Reserve Banking:**

- Banks **lend out money they don't actually have,** making billions in profit from interest while creating economic instability.

☐ **Bailouts for Banks, Foreclosures for People:**

- When ordinary people struggle with debt, they **lose their homes and assets.**

. When banks make reckless financial decisions, **governments bail them out with taxpayer money.**

☐ Who Benefits?

☐ **Bank CEOs & Shareholders:** They profit from loans and investments.

☐ **Real Estate Investors:** They buy foreclosed homes and rent them out at inflated prices.

☐ **Lesson:** The financial system **profits from keeping people in debt—escaping this trap requires financial literacy and strategic action.**

---

3. The Stock Market: A Casino for the Rich

☐ *The stock market is not about "hard work"—it's a game rigged in favor of those who already have wealth.*

☐ How the Stock Market Benefits the Wealthy

☐ **Corporate Buybacks:** Companies spend billions buying back their own stocks to inflate prices—benefiting shareholders, not workers.

☐ **Insider Trading & Political Corruption:** The elite receive **privileged financial information** before the public does.

☐ **401(k) and Pension Scams:** Many retirement plans **depend on stock market stability,** which is **highly manipulated.**

☐ Example: The 2008 Financial Crisis

. Banks **caused the crisis through reckless investments.**

. Millions of people lost their homes, while **banks got government bailouts.**

. **The rich bought up cheap real estate,** further consolidating their wealth.

☐ **Lesson:** The stock market **isn't designed to create wealth for everyone—it's a tool for the elite to extract wealth from the economy.**

---

4. Corporate Monopolies: Controlling the Economy

⬛ The world's largest corporations do not compete—they collaborate to dominate industries and crush small businesses.

⬛ **How Corporations Rig the System**

⬛ **Monopoly Power:** A few giant corporations own most industries (Big Tech, Big Pharma, Big Banks, etc.), leaving consumers with **no real choice.**

⬛ **Low Wages, High Prices:** Companies **pay workers the bare minimum while increasing prices for maximum profit.**

⬛ **Political Influence:** Corporations **fund politicians** to ensure laws benefit them, not workers.

⬛ **Example: The Amazon Effect**

- Amazon **kills small businesses** by underpricing competitors, then raises prices once it dominates the market.

- Workers **earn low wages** while Amazon executives become billionaires.

⬛ **Lesson:** Corporate monopolies **crush competition and extract wealth from the working class.**

---

5. The Tax System: A Rigged Game for the Rich

⬛ The tax system is not about fairness—it's about making sure the wealthy pay less while the poor pay more.

⬛ **How the Wealthy Avoid Taxes**

⬛ **Offshore Tax Havens:** Billionaires hide money in **Cayman Islands, Switzerland, and Panama** to avoid paying taxes.

⬛ **Corporate Tax Loopholes:** Many multinational companies **pay little to no taxes** despite making billions in profit.

⬛ **Capital Gains Tax Advantage:** The rich make most of their money through investments, which are **taxed at lower rates than wages.**

⬛ **Who Pays the Most Taxes?**

◻ **The working class:** Pays high payroll taxes, income taxes, and sales taxes.
◻ **The middle class:** Often trapped in a bracket that prevents upward mobility.
◻ **The wealthy:** Use lawyers and loopholes to avoid taxation.

◻ **Lesson:** The tax system is structured to **burden workers while protecting the wealth of the elite.**

---

6. The Real Estate Scam: Why Housing is Unaffordable

◻ *Housing is a basic human need—but it has been turned into an investment game for the wealthy.*

◻ **How the Housing Market is Rigged**

◻ **Wall Street Investment in Housing:** Hedge funds buy up properties, raising rents and pricing out first-time homebuyers.
◻ **Gentrification:** Lower-income residents are displaced as wealthy investors **inflate property values.**
◻ **Mortgage Debt Traps:** Homebuyers end up **paying for decades** while banks profit from interest.

◻ **Example: The 2008 Housing Crash**

- Banks **gave out bad loans**, then crashed the economy.
- Ordinary homeowners **lost everything**, while **investors bought their properties at a discount.**

◻ **Lesson:** The housing market is designed **not for affordability, but for profit.**

---

7. How to Break Free from Financial Exploitation

◻ *Escaping economic control requires strategic action, financial literacy, and collective effort.*

◻ **Steps to Take for Financial Independence**

✓ **Avoid Unnecessary Debt:** Credit cards, payday loans, and student loans **trap people in long-term financial servitude.**
✓ **Invest in Assets, Not Liabilities:** Buy property, stocks, or

start a business instead of spending on consumer goods.

✓ **Support Worker-Owned Businesses:** Cooperatives give power to employees rather than corporate executives.

✓ **Push for Economic Reform:** Demand policies that increase **progressive taxation, break up monopolies, and strengthen labor rights.**

✓ **Organize for Change:** Support **labor unions, wealth** redistribution policies, and economic justice movements.

☐ **Lesson:** The financial system is rigged—but by understanding its mechanisms, **you can reclaim financial power.**

Final Thought: Money is Power—Who Controls It?

☐ **The financial system is not neutral—it is a tool used by the elite to maintain control.**

☐ **Debt, taxation, corporate monopolies, and stock markets are all designed to extract wealth from the working class.**

☐ **To break free, you must understand the system, fight for reform, and take control of your own financial future.**

The question is not whether the system is fair—the question is, what will you do to escape it? ☐

CHAPTER 26: THE IMPORTANCE OF FINANCIAL LITERACY FOR EMPOWERMENT

"If you don't learn how money works, you will always be working for someone who does."

Financial literacy is one of the most powerful tools for individual and collective empowerment. Yet, the education system rarely teaches people how to manage money, build wealth, or escape financial traps. This is not an accident—a financially educated population is harder to manipulate, exploit, and control.

This chapter explores **why financial literacy is essential, how the system keeps people ignorant about money, and the key financial skills every citizen needs to break free from economic control.**

---

1. What is Financial Literacy and Why is it So Important?

☐ *Financial literacy is the ability to understand and manage money effectively.*

☐ **Key Aspects of Financial Literacy**

☐ **Budgeting & Money Management** – Knowing how to **track expenses and live within your means.**

☐ **Debt Management** – Understanding **good debt vs. bad debt** and how to avoid financial traps.

☐ **Investing & Wealth Building** – Learning how to **make money work for you instead of just working for money.**

☐ **Understanding Inflation & Taxes** – Knowing how policies affect your income and financial stability.

☐ **Entrepreneurship & Passive Income** – Learning how to **create income streams that don't depend on wages.**

☐ **Lesson:** Financial literacy is about **control—either you control your money, or the system controls you.**

---

2. How the System Keeps People Financially Illiterate

☐ *If people don't understand money, they remain dependent on banks, corporations, and the government.*

☐ **Tactics Used to Keep Citizens Financially Ignorant**

☐ **No Financial Education in Schools:** Schools teach algebra but not how to pay taxes or invest.

☐ **Debt Normalization:** Society teaches people to **borrow money for college, homes, and cars** without explaining how debt traps work.

☐ **Media Distraction:** Financial success is shown as **luxury consumption (cars, clothes, vacations)** instead of real wealth-building (assets, investments).

☐ **Paycheck-to-Paycheck Culture:** Wages are set **just high enough to survive but not enough to escape the system.**

☐ **Lesson:** The system benefits from **financially illiterate citizens** who rely on banks, loans, and wages rather than **owning assets and creating wealth.**

---

3. How Financial Literacy Leads to Freedom

Money doesn't buy happiness, but it does buy freedom from exploitation.

Why Financial Literacy is Empowering

Reduces Dependence on Employers – You don't have to tolerate abusive jobs if you have savings and investments.

Prevents Debt Slavery – Understanding credit, interest rates, and loans keeps you from financial traps.

Increases Political & Social Power – Wealth gives you the ability to support causes, start businesses, and fund movements.

Improves Mental Health – Financial security reduces stress, anxiety, and burnout.

Lesson: When you understand money, **you gain choices, control, and confidence in your future.**

---

4. Essential Financial Skills for Personal Empowerment

Master these skills, and you will never be financially trapped.

1. Budgeting & Expense Tracking

- Keep **a written or digital budget** of your income and expenses.
- Follow the **50/30/20 rule:**
  - **50% Needs (Rent, Bills, Food)**
  - **30% Wants (Entertainment, Travel)**
  - **20% Savings & Investments**

2. Avoiding & Managing Debt

- **Good Debt** = Student loans (if used wisely), mortgages, business investments.
- **Bad Debt** = Credit cards, payday loans, car loans with high interest.
- **Rule: Never borrow money for depreciating assets**

(cars, electronics, vacations).

3. Saving & Emergency Funds

- **Goal:** Save at least **3-6 months of living expenses** in a high-interest account.
- **Pay Yourself First:** Treat savings as a non-negotiable bill.

4. Investing & Passive Income

- **Invest in Assets:** Stocks, real estate, small businesses, or retirement accounts.
- **Multiple Income Streams:** Side businesses, dividend stocks, rental properties.
- **Compounding Interest:** Start early—money grows exponentially over time.

5. Understanding Inflation & Taxes

- Learn how **inflation eats away at savings**—invest instead of just saving.
- Know **how taxes work**—take advantage of deductions, tax credits, and tax-free investment accounts.

 Lesson: Financial literacy is not just about **saving money—it's about growing money and escaping financial dependency.**

---

5. The Role of Financial Independence in Challenging the System

 The system keeps people struggling financially so they don't have time, energy, or resources to challenge it.

 Why the Elite Fear Financially Empowered Citizens

 Workers with savings don't tolerate exploitation.

 Debt-free citizens can take risks, start businesses, and organize for change.

 The financially literate can see through economic lies and corruption.

 Wealthy citizens can influence politics instead of just surviving.

 Lesson: Financial empowerment is not just personal—it is **a revolutionary act against economic oppression.**

---

6. Community-Based Financial Empowerment: How to Help Others Break Free

 True financial empowerment comes when communities work together.

 How to Spread Financial Literacy

✓ **Teach Friends & Family** – Share books, videos, and courses on money management.
✓ **Form Investment & Savings Groups** – Pool resources to invest in real estate, businesses, or community projects.
✓ **Support Local Businesses** – Stop enriching corporate monopolies—invest in your own community.
✓ **Advocate for Financial Education in Schools** – Demand real financial training for students.

 Examples of Successful Community Financial Movements

 Cooperative Businesses: Workers own the company instead of corporate executives.
 Local Investment Funds: Community members fund small businesses instead of big banks.
 Credit Unions: People bank with institutions that reinvest in the local economy.

 Lesson: Financial power must be shared, not just hoarded—strong communities create strong individuals.

---

7. How to Start Your Financial Freedom Journey Today

 Breaking free from financial control doesn't happen overnight—but small steps make a big difference.

 Action Plan for Financial Independence

✓ **Track Your Spending** – Start a budget today.

✓ **Cut Bad Debt** – Pay off high-interest credit cards and loans.

✓ **Save for Emergencies** – Set up an emergency fund (even $500 is a start).

✓ **Start Investing** – Even $50 a month in an index fund grows over time.

✓ **Learn More** – Read books, watch financial literacy videos, and follow experts.

✓ **Find a Mentor** – Someone who understands money can help you avoid mistakes.

 Lesson: You don't need to be rich to be financially free—you just need knowledge, discipline, and a plan.

Final Thought: Financial Freedom is the Ultimate Power

 Money is not just about luxury—it is about control, freedom, and opportunity.

 The system benefits when people are financially dependent—break free by educating yourself.

 When enough people take control of their financial future, the system of economic oppression starts to crumble.

The question is not whether you can be financially free—the question is, will you take the first step?

CHAPTER 27: STEPS FOR ECONOMIC INDEPENDENCE AND RESISTANCE AGAINST EXPLOITATION

"The system thrives when people remain financially dependent. Real freedom begins when you take control of your financial future."

E conomic independence is more than just having money —it is about escaping financial traps, resisting corporate exploitation, and building personal and community wealth. The system is designed to keep people in a cycle of low wages, high debt, and financial dependence, but by taking strategic action, individuals can break free and reclaim their power.

This chapter outlines **practical steps to achieve economic independence, resist financial exploitation, and create long-term security.**

1. Understand the System: Recognizing Economic Exploitation

You cannot break free from a system you don't understand.

The Core Problems

Wages Stay Low, Costs Keep Rising – The economy is structured to keep workers struggling while corporations make record profits.

Debt is a Trap – The financial system encourages borrowing but makes repayment difficult.

Jobs Are Insecure by Design – Companies keep workers replaceable to prevent power or stability.

Consumerism Keeps You Broke – Society pressures people to spend money they don't have on things they don't need.

Who Benefits from Economic Exploitation?

- **Banks & Lenders** – Make billions from high-interest debt.

- **Corporations** – Keep wages low while maximizing shareholder profits.

- **Politicians** – Protect the wealthy elite while making people believe they have economic opportunity.

Lesson: The first step toward financial independence is realizing **the game is rigged—but you can still play smarter.**

2. Eliminate Debt: Free Yourself from Financial Chains

Debt is the modern form of slavery—escape it, and you gain power over your future.

How to Get Out of Debt

✓ **Stop Accumulating New Debt** – Avoid credit card debt, payday loans, and unnecessary borrowing.

✓ **Prioritize High-Interest Debt** – Pay off credit cards, personal loans, and payday loans first.

✓ **Negotiate & Consolidate** – Call lenders and ask for lower interest rates or better repayment plans.

✓ **Use the Snowball or Avalanche Method:**

- **Snowball Method:** Pay off the smallest debt first for psychological wins.
- **Avalanche Method:** Pay off the highest-interest debt first to save more money.

 Lesson: Debt keeps you trapped—**the faster you eliminate it, the sooner you reclaim financial freedom.**

---

3. Build an Emergency Fund: Create Financial Security

 If you don't have savings, one emergency can push you back into financial dependence.

How to Build an Emergency Fund

✓ **Start Small:** Save **at least $500–$1,000** to cover unexpected expenses.

✓ **Set a Goal:** Aim for **3–6 months' worth of living expenses** in savings.

✓ **Keep It Accessible:** Use a **high-interest savings account** instead of risky investments.

✓ **Automate Savings:** Set up an automatic transfer to savings every month.

 Lesson: Financial independence starts with **security—an emergency fund prevents you from falling back into debt.**

---

4. Stop Living Paycheck to Paycheck: Master Budgeting

 If you don't control your money, someone else will.

How to Take Control of Your Finances

✓ **Track Every Dollar:** Use budgeting apps like **YNAB, Mint, or EveryDollar.**

✓ **Follow the 50/30/20 Rule:**

- **50% Needs (Rent, Bills, Food)**
- **30% Wants (Entertainment, Travel)**

- **20% Savings & Investments**
  ✓ **Reduce Unnecessary Spending:** Cut subscriptions, impulse purchases, and eating out.
  ✓ **Use Cash Instead of Credit:** If you can't afford it **without a credit card, don't buy it.**

☐ **Lesson:** Budgeting is not about restriction—it's about **directing your money toward freedom instead of financial traps.**

---

5. Invest & Build Wealth: Escape the Cycle of Wage Dependence

☐ *Wealth is built by owning assets, not just earning wages.*

☐ **Where to Start Investing**

✓ **Stock Market (Long-Term Growth):** Invest in **index funds, ETFs, or dividend stocks** instead of chasing trends.
✓ **Real Estate (Passive Income):** Save for **rental properties or REITs (Real Estate Investment Trusts).**
✓ **Side Businesses (Multiple Income Streams):** Start **freelancing, consulting, or a small online business.**
✓ **Crypto & Alternative Assets (High-Risk, High-Reward):** Only invest **what you can afford to lose.**

☐ **Rules for Smart Investing**

☐ **Start Early:** Even small investments grow significantly over time.

☐ **Be Consistent:** Invest monthly, no matter how small the amount.

☐ **Avoid Get-Rich-Quick Schemes:** If it sounds too good to be true, it is.

☐ **Lesson:** The financially independent **don't rely on wages alone —they make their money work for them.**

---

6. Resist Corporate Exploitation: Reclaim Economic Power

☐ *Corporations exploit workers through low wages, bad conditions, and job insecurity—fight back.*

⬚ How to Fight Workplace Exploitation

✓ **Join a Union:** Collective bargaining leads to better pay and job protections.

✓ **Negotiate Your Salary:** Don't accept the first offer—always ask for more.

✓ **Develop Skills That Increase Your Value:** Learn **high-income skills (coding, marketing, sales, investing, etc.).**

✓ **Don't Be Afraid to Quit:** If a job exploits you, **find a better one or start your own business.**

⬚ **Lesson:** Corporations thrive on worker dependence—**the less you need them, the more power you have.**

---

7. Build Economic Resistance in Your Community

⬚ *Individual financial freedom is important, but collective financial power changes societies.*

⬚ How to Strengthen Community Economic Resistance

✓ **Support Local Businesses:** Keep money in the community instead of funding corporate monopolies.

✓ **Invest in Worker-Owned Cooperatives:** Businesses owned by employees create long-term economic security.

✓ **Share Financial Knowledge:** Teach family and friends how to escape financial traps.

✓ **Organize for Economic Justice:** Push for **higher wages, fair taxation, and better financial regulations.**

⬚ **Lesson:** A strong community economy **reduces reliance on corporations and empowers individuals.**

---

8. Use Political Action to Challenge Economic Inequality

⬚ *The economy is not just personal—it is political. The rules are written to benefit the elite, but they can be changed.*

⬚ What to Fight For

✓ **Higher Wages & Worker Protections** – Minimum wage increases, universal healthcare, and labor rights.

✓ **Wealth Tax & Corporate Regulation** – Closing tax loopholes and breaking up monopolies.

✓ **Debt Forgiveness & Financial Reform** – Student loan cancellation, lower interest rates, and public banking options.

☐ **Lesson:** Economic independence isn't just about personal wealth—it's about **changing the system for everyone.**

Final Thought: Freedom is Built on Economic Power

☐ **If you control your money, you control your future. If the system controls your money, it controls you.**

☐ **Achieving financial independence is not just personal success—it is resistance against economic exploitation.**

☐ **When enough people break free, the system must change.**

The question is not whether economic independence is possible—the question is, will you take the first step? ☐

PART FOUR: RECLAIMING POWER AS AN ORDINARY CITIZEN

CHAPTER 28:
THE POWER OF
COLLECTIVE ACTION

"Alone, we are vulnerable. Together, we are unstoppable."

T hroughout history, real change has never come from politicians, corporations, or elites—it has always been driven by ordinary people coming together to challenge oppression. From civil rights to labor movements, from political revolutions to economic boycotts, collective action has been the most effective force for transformation.

This chapter explores **how ordinary citizens can reclaim power through unity, grassroots organizing, and mass mobilization.**

---

1. Why Collective Action Works

⬜ *The system is built to make individuals feel powerless—but when people unite, they become a force too strong to ignore.*

⬜ **The Power of the People**

⬜ **Mass Movements Cannot Be Ignored** – When millions demand change, governments and corporations are forced to respond.

◻ **Strikes & Boycotts Hit the System Where It Hurts** – Economic pressure forces the powerful to listen.

◻ **Shared Knowledge Strengthens Movements** – When people educate each other, misinformation loses its grip.

◻ **Community Support Builds Resilience** – Movements that support their members can sustain long-term action.

◻ **Lesson: The system thrives on division and isolation. When people unite, they become unstoppable.**

---

2. Key Elements of Successful Collective Action

◻ *Not all protests and movements succeed—successful ones follow key strategies.*

◻ **The Four Pillars of Effective Collective Action**

✓ **Organization:** Movements need clear goals, structure, and leadership.

✓ **Persistence:** Real change doesn't happen overnight—consistent pressure is key.

✓ **Economic Disruption:** Strikes, boycotts, and financial pressure make elites take notice.

✓ **Mass Participation:** The more people involved, the greater the impact.

◻ **Example: The Civil Rights Movement (1950s-60s, U.S.)**

◻ **Rosa Parks refused to give up her seat** → **Sparked the Montgomery Bus Boycott**

◻ **The boycott lasted 381 days** → **Bus segregation laws were overturned**

◻ **Mass protests, legal action, and media coverage forced government change**

◻ **Lesson: A single action can spark a movement—but sustained collective pressure forces change.**

---

3. How to Organize a Movement

◻ *Every successful movement follows a step-by-step process to grow and sustain itself.*

☐ Steps to Building an Effective Movement

✓ **Identify the Core Issue:** What problem are you fighting against? (Corruption, inequality, labor exploitation, etc.)

✓ **Educate & Raise Awareness:** Use social media, independent media, and local events to spread the message.

✓ **Build a Strong Network:** Connect with activists, community leaders, and organizations.

✓ **Plan Strategic Actions:** Protests, petitions, strikes, boycotts—target weaknesses in the system.

✓ **Use Media to Amplify the Message:** Engage journalists, create viral content, and control the narrative.

✓ **Sustain Momentum:** Keep people engaged through regular meetings, events, and progress updates.

☐ Example: The Arab Spring (2010-2012)

☐ **Started with a single protest in Tunisia** → Spread to multiple countries

☐ **Social media mobilized millions** → Governments could not control the message

☐ **Mass protests & strikes led to regime changes**

☐ **Lesson: When people are organized, even oppressive governments can be overthrown.**

---

4. Economic Resistance: Strikes, Boycotts & Financial Pressure

☐ *The system depends on economic power—when workers and consumers refuse to comply, it weakens significantly.*

☐ How Economic Resistance Works

☐ **Strikes:** Workers collectively refuse to work until demands are met.

☐ **Boycotts:** Consumers refuse to buy products from unethical companies.

☐ **Divestment Campaigns:** Pressuring investors to pull money from harmful industries.

☐ **Example: The Indian Independence Movement (1930s-40s)**

☐ **Salt March (1930):** Gandhi led thousands in a protest against British salt taxes.

☐ **Mass Boycotts:** Indians refused to buy British goods, crippling colonial profits.

☐ **Result:** Economic pressure forced Britain to grant independence in 1947.

☐ **Lesson: Governments and corporations fear economic resistance because it directly threatens their profits and control.**

---

5. Using Technology & Social Media for Collective Action

☐ *Digital activism is one of the most powerful tools for mobilizing people quickly and globally.*

☐ **How to Leverage Technology for Resistance**

✓ **Social Media Campaigns:** Use platforms like Twitter, Facebook, and TikTok to spread awareness.

✓ **Secure Communication:** Use encrypted messaging apps like Signal and ProtonMail to protect activists.

✓ **Online Petitions & Fundraising:** Organize petitions and raise funds for legal defense, supplies, and logistics.

✓ **Live Streaming & Citizen Journalism:** Document protests and expose government/corporate abuses in real time.

☐ **Example: #MeToo Movement (2017-Present)**

☐ **Social media gave survivors a platform to share their stories.**

☐ **Exposed powerful abusers in Hollywood, politics, and corporations.**

☐ **Forced real policy changes in workplace protections.**

☐ **Lesson: Technology can amplify grassroots movements, bypassing mainstream media control.**

---

6. Overcoming Government & Corporate Suppression

☐ *When collective action becomes powerful, those in control will try to shut it down.*

☐ Tactics Used to Suppress Movements

☐ **Censorship & Misinformation:** Governments spread fake news to discredit activists.

☐ **Surveillance & Arrests:** Authorities monitor and intimidate organizers.

☐ **Divide & Conquer Strategies:** Elites create divisions within movements to weaken them.

☐ How to Counter Suppression

✔ **Stay United:** Do not allow internal divisions to destroy the movement.

✔ **Use Encrypted Communication:** Protect conversations from government surveillance.

✔ **Control the Narrative:** Use alternative media to counter propaganda.

✔ **Have Contingency Plans:** Be prepared for arrests, internet shutdowns, or infiltration.

☐ **Lesson: Movements survive suppression when they adapt, stay organized, and refuse to back down.**

---

7. Turning Protests into Lasting Change

☐ *A protest is only the beginning—real success comes when movements turn into laws, policies, and social transformation.*

☐ Steps to Ensure Long-Term Impact

✔ **Demand Specific Policy Changes:** Movements need clear, achievable goals.

✔ **Build Alliances:** Work with organizations, unions, and legal groups to sustain momentum.

✔ **Engage in the Political Process:** Encourage activists to run for office or push for legislative reforms.

✔ **Maintain Public Pressure:** Governments and corporations will try to wait for movements to die down—don't let them.

☐ **Example: LGBTQ+ Rights Movement**

 Decades of activism led to legal protections and marriage equality.
 Continued pressure forces companies and politicians to adopt inclusive policies.

 Lesson: Protests raise awareness, but sustained action turns demands into reality.

Final Thought: Together, We Are Unstoppable

 No single person can change the system—but when people unite, they can bring down empires.
 History proves that collective action is the most powerful weapon against oppression.
 The system fears an organized, informed, and united population—because that is how real change happens.

The question is not whether collective action works—the question is, will you take part in it?

CHAPTER 29: HOW MOVEMENTS LIKE CIVIL RIGHTS, CLIMATE ACTIVISM, AND WORKERS' RIGHTS SUCCEEDED

"Every great movement started with ordinary people refusing to accept the status quo."

Social, economic, and political justice has never been given freely—it has always been won through organized resistance, collective action, and relentless pressure. Whether it's the civil rights movement, climate activism, or workers' rights struggles, history proves that when people unite, even the most powerful systems can be forced to change.

This chapter examines **how these movements succeeded, what strategies they used, and what lessons modern activists can**

learn from them.

---

1. The Civil Rights Movement: Overcoming Racial Segregation & Discrimination

☐ *The civil rights movement in the U.S. (1950s-1960s) was a fight against racial segregation, police brutality, and voter suppression.*

☐ **Strategies That Led to Success**

☐ **Nonviolent Resistance:** Peaceful protests, sit-ins, and marches drew global attention.

☐ **Economic Boycotts:** The Montgomery Bus Boycott (1955) forced businesses to desegregate.

☐ **Legal Battles:** NAACP lawyers challenged discriminatory laws in courts.

☐ **Media & Public Awareness:** Televised brutality exposed injustice and built national support.

☐ **Key Moments**

☐ **Montgomery Bus Boycott (1955-56)** – Sparked by Rosa Parks' arrest, this 381-day boycott led to desegregation of public transportation.

☐ **March on Washington (1963)** – Over 250,000 people gathered as Martin Luther King Jr. delivered his famous *"I Have a Dream"* speech.

☐ **Civil Rights Act (1964) & Voting Rights Act (1965)** – Forced legal end to segregation and voter suppression.

☐ **Lesson: Nonviolent resistance, economic pressure, and legal action combined to force a system-wide change.**

---

2. Climate Activism: Fighting for the Planet's Future

☐ *Climate activism is one of the largest global movements, challenging corporations and governments to act against climate change.*

☐ **Strategies That Are Making an Impact**

☐ **Global Protests & Strikes:** Millions participate in climate strikes, demanding policy action.

- **Corporate Accountability Campaigns:** Pressuring fossil fuel companies and banks to divest from dirty energy.
- **Legal Battles:** Activists sue governments and corporations for environmental destruction.
- **Scientific Data & Public Awareness:** Climate activists use scientific evidence to challenge misinformation.

Key Moments

- **Paris Agreement (2015)** – International commitment to limit global warming, influenced by activist pressure.
- **Fridays for Future (2018-Present)** – Youth-led school strikes for climate action, initiated by Greta Thunberg.
- **Standing Rock Protests (2016-2017)** – Indigenous-led movement against the Dakota Access Pipeline succeeded in halting construction (temporarily).

Lesson: Climate activism works when it combines mass mobilization, legal action, and economic pressure on polluters.

---

3. Workers' Rights Movement: Winning Fair Wages & Safe Conditions

The fight for workers' rights—from the 8-hour workday to minimum wage laws—was won through strikes, unions, and collective bargaining.

Strategies That Led to Success

Strikes & Walkouts: Workers refused to work until conditions improved.

Unionization: Labor unions fought for better wages, benefits, and protections.

Legislative Pressure: Activists demanded laws to prevent worker exploitation.

Public Awareness & Media Campaigns: Exposed dangerous working conditions to gain public sympathy.

Key Moments

◻ **Haymarket Affair (1886)** – Mass protests led to the 8-hour workday becoming a standard.
◻ **The New Deal (1930s, U.S.)** – Worker activism pushed Franklin D. Roosevelt to pass labor protections.
◻ **Amazon & Starbucks Unionization (2020s)** – New waves of strikes and organizing are forcing major corporations to negotiate with workers.

◻ **Lesson: Strikes, unions, and legislative pressure have been the most effective tools in securing workers' rights.**

---

4. Lessons from Successful Movements

◻ *All major movements share common tactics that make them effective.*

◻ **Key Strategies for Any Movement**

✔ **Mass Participation:** The more people involved, the harder it is to ignore.
✔ **Economic Pressure:** Boycotts, strikes, and financial disruption force change.
✔ **Legal Action:** Courts can be used to challenge unjust laws and policies.
✔ **Public Awareness:** Media coverage and social media amplify the message.
✔ **Persistence:** Movements must endure beyond one protest—change takes time.

◻ **Lesson: Powerful institutions do not change unless they are forced to—consistent pressure is the only way to win.**

Final Thought: The Future Belongs to Those Who Take Action

◻ **Ordinary people have always been the force behind major societal changes.**
◻ **Whether it's racial justice, climate action, or workers' rights, history proves that when enough people resist, the system must respond.**
◻ **The question is not whether movements can succeed—the**

question is, will you be part of the next one? □

CHAPTER 30: THE STRATEGY OF UNITY: HOW SMALL EFFORTS COMBINE INTO MASSIVE CHANGE

"A single drop of water is weak, but an ocean is unstoppable."

Throughout history, real change has never come from a single person—it has come from the collective efforts of many. The most successful movements were not built overnight but were the result of small, strategic actions accumulating into massive, undeniable forces.

This chapter explores **how unity transforms scattered efforts into powerful change, the tactics used to unite people, and how individuals can contribute to movements that shake the system.**

---

1. Why Unity is the Strongest Strategy for Change

☐ *The system is designed to divide people—because divided people cannot resist oppression.*

☐ The Power of Collective Action

☐ **Numbers Give Legitimacy** – When thousands or millions of people demand change, their voices become impossible to ignore.

☐ **Mass Participation Increases Impact** – More people means more pressure on governments, corporations, and institutions.

☐ **Collaboration Brings Strengths Together** – Movements succeed when people bring different skills (organizing, legal, media, tech, etc.).

☐ **Sustained Effort Creates Lasting Change** – A movement that grows in numbers and persistence forces real shifts in power.

☐ **Lesson: No single person or action wins a fight, but united small efforts can move mountains.**

---

2. How Small Actions Build a Movement

☐ *Movements don't start as massive forces—they begin with small, consistent actions that inspire others to join.*

☐ Steps to Grow a Movement from Small to Powerful

✓ **One Person Speaks Out:** Every movement starts with someone challenging injustice (e.g., Rosa Parks refusing to give up her seat).

✓ **A Small Group Takes Action:** Others support the cause, forming the foundation of the movement.

✓ **Community Engagement Expands Influence:** Social media, protests, and word of mouth attract more supporters.

✓ **Momentum Forces Public Awareness:** Media coverage and viral campaigns make the issue unavoidable.

✓ **Mass Participation Creates Pressure:** Once the movement reaches a critical mass, institutions are forced to respond.

☐ **Example: The #MeToo Movement (2017-Present)**

☐ **One person (Tarana Burke) started the movement.**

🞐 A few brave individuals spoke out against workplace harassment.

🞐 More survivors came forward, forcing major companies to address abuse.

🞐 The movement led to new policies and the downfall of powerful abusers.

🞐 Lesson: Every major movement started as a small act of defiance that inspired others to join.

3. Overcoming Division: Uniting People Across Differences

🞐 *Governments and corporations use division as a strategy to weaken collective action—resisting this is key to success.*

🞐 Common Tactics Used to Divide People

🞐 **Political Polarization:** Making people believe that those on the "other side" are the enemy, instead of the corrupt system itself.

🞐 **Racial & Class Divisions:** Keeping poor and working-class communities divided prevents them from challenging economic exploitation.

🞐 **Disinformation & Propaganda:** Media manipulation creates distrust and confusion within movements.

🞐 How to Build Unity Despite Differences

✓ **Find Common Ground:** Focus on shared goals (e.g., economic justice, human rights, climate action) instead of small differences.

✓ **Encourage Open Dialogue:** Avoid unnecessary ideological purity tests that exclude potential allies.

✓ **Use Inclusive Messaging:** Make it clear that the movement welcomes people from all backgrounds.

✓ **Avoid Internal Conflicts:** Keep the focus on fighting the system, not each other.

🞐 **Lesson: The system fears unity because when the people stand together, they cannot be controlled.**

4. The Role of Networks & Decentralized Organization

 Hierarchical movements can be crushed—decentralized movements are harder to stop.

 Why Decentralized Movements Succeed

 No Single Leader Can Be Taken Down – If leadership is spread out, governments cannot silence the movement by targeting one person.

 Local Groups Work Independently – Small, autonomous groups allow activism to continue even if one area is suppressed.

 Flexible & Adaptable Strategies – Decentralized structures allow for quick responses to changing situations.

 Example: The Anonymous Hacktivist Movement

 No central leadership—just shared goals of exposing corruption and oppression.

 Multiple small groups operate independently, making it impossible to shut down completely.

 Actions range from digital protests to leaks exposing government misconduct.

 Lesson: A movement with many leaders and independent branches is stronger than one with a single point of failure.

---

5. Digital Activism: Using Technology to Unite People Globally

 The internet has changed activism—movements can now spread across borders instantly.

 How to Use Digital Tools for Mass Mobilization

 ✓ **Social Media Campaigns:** Hashtags, viral videos, and online petitions can mobilize millions.

 ✓ **Secure Communication Platforms:** Apps like Signal and ProtonMail help activists coordinate safely.

 ✓ **Live Streaming & Citizen Journalism:** Exposing government or corporate abuses in real-time forces accountability.

 ✓ **Hacktivism & Cyber Resistance:** Digital activism can disrupt oppressive systems and expose corruption.

 Example: The Arab Spring (2010-2012)

 Social media helped organize protests in Egypt, Tunisia, and Libya.
 Videos of police violence exposed human rights abuses.
 The rapid spread of information made government propaganda ineffective.

 Lesson: Digital tools allow ordinary people to challenge oppressive power structures on a global scale.

6. Economic Disruption: How Consumer & Labor Power Forces Change

 The system depends on people's labor and spending—if we withdraw these, it weakens.

 Tactics That Use Economic Power Against Oppression

 Strikes: Workers refusing to work forces businesses to meet demands.
 Boycotts: Consumers refusing to buy from unethical companies pressures them to change.
 Buycotts: Supporting ethical businesses instead of exploitative corporations shifts wealth toward fairer systems.
 Alternative Economies: Community-based trade and worker cooperatives reduce reliance on exploitative markets.

 Example: The Montgomery Bus Boycott (1955-1956)

 Black Americans stopped using segregated buses for over a year.
 The economic loss forced companies to desegregate.
 The movement became a model for future civil rights actions.

 Lesson: Withholding economic participation is one of the most powerful ways to force systemic change.

7. Sustaining a Movement: Keeping Momentum & Avoiding Burnout

Movements often fail not because they are wrong, but because they lose energy—staying engaged is key to winning.

How to Keep a Movement Alive

✓ **Celebrate Small Wins:** Progress keeps people motivated.

✓ **Avoid Activist Burnout:** Organizers need to rest and support each other.

✓ **Educate the Next Generation:** Teach young people about activism so movements continue beyond one generation.

✓ **Adapt Strategies as Needed:** Be flexible—if one method stops working, try another.

Example: The LGBTQ+ Rights Movement

 Took decades, but persistence led to legal victories worldwide.

 Generations of activists built upon past efforts to push forward.

 Lesson: Long-term movements win because they refuse to stop until they succeed.

Final Thought: Small Actions, Big Impact

 No movement begins as a giant force—it grows from small, strategic actions that inspire others to join.

 When ordinary people unite, they can break oppressive systems, challenge corrupt power, and reshape the world.

 The question is not whether unity works—the question is, will you take part in it?

CHAPTER 31: THE ROLE OF DIGITAL COMMUNITIES IN MOBILIZING PEOPLE

"The revolution will not only be televised—it will be live-streamed, tweeted, and shared worldwide."

The internet has transformed activism. Movements that once took years to organize can now mobilize millions in days. Digital communities have become the new battleground for social change, offering activists tools to spread awareness, coordinate protests, and challenge oppressive systems in real-time.

This chapter explores **how digital communities are reshaping activism, the tactics used for mobilization, and how ordinary people can use online platforms to reclaim power.**

1. How Digital Communities Empower Movements

☐ *The internet has removed barriers to organizing—now, anyone with a smartphone can be part of a global movement.*

Why Digital Communities Are So Powerful

Instant Communication: Activists can organize and respond to events in real-time.

Mass Awareness: Information spreads rapidly, exposing injustice and corruption.

Borderless Activism: A protest in one country can gain global support.

Decentralized Organization: No single leader can be targeted—movements grow organically.

Empowerment of the Ordinary Citizen: People who once felt powerless can now contribute to change with a tweet, video, or petition.

Lesson: Social media has shifted the power dynamic—activists can now control the narrative, not just governments and corporations.

---

2. Social Media as a Tool for Mobilization

Hashtags are the new protest banners, and viral videos are the new frontline reports.

How Social Media Fuels Activism

✓ **Hashtag Movements:** Viral hashtags unite people under a common cause (#MeToo, #BlackLivesMatter, #FridaysForFuture).

✓ **Live Streaming Protests:** Bypasses mainstream media and exposes police brutality and government crackdowns.

✓ **Online Petitions & Fundraising:** Platforms like Change.org and GoFundMe empower grassroots action.

✓ **Anonymous Organizing:** Encrypted apps allow activists to plan without government interference.

Example: The Arab Spring (2010-2012)

Social media platforms like Facebook and Twitter helped organize protests.

Videos of police brutality went viral, gaining international

attention.

❒ **Governments tried to shut down the internet, proving its power in mobilization.**

❒ **Lesson: Social media is not just for sharing opinions—it is a tool for organizing real-world action.**

---

3. The Role of Online Communities in Spreading Awareness

❒ *Before people take action, they must first become aware of the issue —digital communities make this happen at an unprecedented scale.*

❒ **How Online Communities Educate & Inspire Action**

❒ **Independent Media:** YouTubers, bloggers, and citizen journalists expose corruption and misinformation.

❒ **Digital Activist Networks:** Reddit, Discord, and Facebook groups connect people with shared causes.

❒ **Crowdsourced Information:** Online forums allow users to share real-time updates on protests, strikes, and government actions.

❒ **Whistleblower Platforms:** Sites like WikiLeaks expose government and corporate crimes.

❒ **Example: The #MeToo Movement (2017-Present)**

❒ **Survivors of sexual harassment shared their stories online.**

❒ **Millions joined the conversation, forcing corporations and governments to take action.**

❒ **Public figures were held accountable, and new policies were implemented.**

❒ **Lesson: Digital communities turn private struggles into global movements.**

---

4. Overcoming Censorship & Digital Suppression

❒ *Governments and corporations fear the power of digital activism— so they try to silence it.*

❒ **Tactics Used to Suppress Online Activism**

Censorship & Platform Bans: Governments block websites and remove activist accounts.

Internet Shutdowns: Authoritarian regimes shut down the internet during protests.

Misinformation Campaigns: Fake news and propaganda are used to discredit movements.

Surveillance & Data Tracking: Governments monitor activists using AI and spyware.

How to Resist Digital Suppression

✓ Use Encrypted Communication: Apps like Signal and ProtonMail protect messages from government surveillance.

✓ Decentralized Platforms: Use blockchain-based or alternative social media like Mastodon.

✓ Virtual Private Networks (VPNs): Bypass government censorship by masking your location.

✓ Mirror Sites & Offline Distribution: Make copies of censored content and distribute it in other formats.

Example: The Hong Kong Protests (2019-2020)

Protesters used encrypted apps to avoid surveillance.

Anonymous forums helped coordinate large-scale demonstrations.

Activists spread information internationally to counter government propaganda.

Lesson: Digital activism requires digital defense—knowing how to protect your information is as important as spreading it.

---

5. The Future of Digital Resistance

Technology is evolving—activists must stay ahead of the system's attempts to suppress them.

Emerging Digital Activism Trends

Decentralized Social Networks: Platforms like Mastodon and Matrix reduce corporate and government control.

◻ **AI-Powered Fact-Checking:** New tools detect fake news and propaganda in real-time.
◻ **Blockchain-Based Whistleblowing:** Secure methods for exposing corruption without being traced.
◻ **Hacker Activism ("Hacktivism"):** Groups like Anonymous target oppressive institutions.

◻ **Example: Hacktivist Collective Anonymous**

◻ **Exposed government corruption and corporate exploitation.**
◻ **Used cyberattacks to disrupt authoritarian regimes.**
◻ **Protected activists by leaking classified information.**

◻ **Lesson: Technology can either be a tool of control or a weapon of resistance—the choice is ours.**

---

6. How to Get Involved in Digital Activism

◻ *You don't need to be a politician, lawyer, or journalist to make a difference—anyone can contribute to online activism.*

◻ **Ways to Participate**

✓ **Share & Amplify Important Information:** Use your platform to spread awareness.
✓ **Support Independent Media & Whistleblowers:** Donate or subscribe to ethical journalists.
✓ **Educate Yourself & Others:** Learn about digital security, fact-checking, and censorship resistance.
✓ **Join Online Activist Networks:** Participate in groups that align with your cause.
✓ **Develop Digital Skills:** Coding, hacking, video editing, and writing can all support activism.

◻ **Lesson: Digital activism is not just for tech experts— everyone has a role to play in spreading awareness and resisting oppression.**

Final Thought: The Revolution is Digital & Global

◻ **Governments and corporations want to control the internet** because they know its power to mobilize people.

◻ The internet has made activism more accessible than ever—anyone can take part.

◻ The system fears an informed, organized, and connected population—because that is how real change happens.

The question is not whether digital activism works—the question is, will you use it to fight for change? ◻

CHAPTER 32: EVERYDAY ACTS THAT CHANGE THE WORLD

"You don't need millions of dollars or a famous name to change the world. You just need the courage to take action —one step at a time."

The greatest movements in history were not led by superheroes or wealthy elites—they were built by ordinary people making small, consistent efforts that added up to massive change. Activism does not always require protests or political power; sometimes, the most effective way to challenge the system is through everyday actions that inspire others, shift culture, and create long-term impact.

This chapter explores **how small, daily choices can create powerful change and how ordinary citizens can reclaim power through consistent action.**

1. The Myth That "Only Big Actions Matter"

☐ *People often believe that change only comes from big, dramatic events. In reality, it's small, everyday actions that make the biggest difference over time.*

☐ Why Small Actions Matter

☐ **They Are Sustainable:** You don't need extreme sacrifices to make an impact—just consistency.

☐ **They Inspire Others:** When one person takes action, others are encouraged to do the same.

☐ **They Weaken the System's Control:** Small disruptions add up to larger systemic shifts.

☐ **They Build Collective Power:** Millions of people making small choices create unstoppable movements.

☐ **Lesson: Change happens when enough people commit to small but meaningful actions.**

---

2. Everyday Actions That Shift Power

☐ *You don't have to wait for a revolution—your daily choices can weaken oppressive systems and strengthen communities.*

☐ Economic Resistance: Vote with Your Wallet

✔ **Boycott Corporations That Exploit Workers & the Environment** – Choose ethical, local, or worker-owned businesses instead.

✔ **Support Independent Media & Artists** – Fund creators who challenge mainstream narratives.

✔ **Buy Secondhand or Repair Instead of Supporting Fast Fashion** – Reduce waste and resist consumer culture.

✔ **Bank with Ethical Institutions** – Switch to credit unions or community banks instead of predatory big banks.

☐ **Impact: Every dollar spent (or withheld) shapes the economy —small shifts in spending habits force corporations to change.**

☐ Political Action: Engage in the System, Even in Small Ways

✔ **Vote in Local Elections** – City councils, school boards, and district attorneys have more daily impact than national leaders.

✔ **Call or Email Your Representatives** – Even a handful of messages can pressure politicians to take action.

✓ **Attend Town Halls & Public Meetings** – Speak up on policies that affect your community.

✓ **Support Grassroots Candidates** – Fund or volunteer for people who represent real change.

❑ **Impact: Small political actions add up—consistent pressure can shift policies and laws.**

❑ Community Building: Strengthen Local Networks

✓ **Join or Start a Mutual Aid Group** – Help neighbors with food, medical care, and housing support.

✓ **Organize Local Skill-Sharing Events** – Teach and learn survival skills, financial literacy, and activism strategies.

✓ **Create Safe Spaces for Dialogue** – Encourage respectful discussions on difficult issues to break down division.

✓ **Support Small, Local Farms & Co-Ops** – Keep food systems out of corporate control.

❑ **Impact: A strong local community is harder to manipulate, control, or exploit.**

❑ Digital Resistance: Use Technology for Change

✓ **Amplify Important Voices** – Share content from activists, whistleblowers, and independent journalists.

✓ **Fact-Check & Combat Misinformation** – Educate people on how to recognize propaganda.

✓ **Support Ethical Tech Alternatives** – Use encrypted messaging, decentralized social media, and privacy-focused platforms.

✓ **Learn & Teach Digital Security** – Help others protect themselves from surveillance and censorship.

❑ **Impact: Controlling your own digital space weakens corporate and government influence over information.**

❑ Environmental Action: Small Choices for a Big Impact

✓ **Reduce Waste & Consumption** – Avoid single-use plastics and unnecessary purchases.

✓ **Switch to Renewable Energy When Possible** – Even small reductions in fossil fuel usage make a difference.

✓ **Grow Your Own Food or Support Local Farmers** – Reduce reliance on industrial agriculture.

✓ **Pressure Companies & Governments for Sustainability Policies** – Collective consumer action forces industry-wide changes.

□ **Impact: Environmental change happens when millions make small but conscious choices every day.**

---

3. The Ripple Effect: How One Action Inspires Another

□ *One person's actions may seem small, but they inspire others to take action, creating a powerful chain reaction.*

□ **Real-World Examples of the Ripple Effect**

□ **Greta Thunberg started skipping school on Fridays to protest climate change** → Inspired millions of students worldwide to join.

□ **A single worker organizing a union at Starbucks** → Led to a national movement for labor rights.

□ **People switching to reusable bags and water bottles** → Pressured corporations to reduce plastic waste.

□ **Lesson: Even the smallest action can trigger massive social shifts when enough people join in.**

---

4. Overcoming Doubt & Inaction

□ *Many people feel like their efforts won't matter—this is exactly what the system wants you to believe.*

□ **Common Excuses That Keep People from Taking Action**

□ **"I'm Just One Person"** → But movements are built by individuals.

□ **"It Won't Change Anything"** → But history proves that

persistence creates real shifts.

□ **"I Don't Have Time"** → But small, everyday actions fit into any lifestyle.

□ **"I Don't Know Where to Start"** → Start small—choose one action that aligns with your values.

□ **Lesson: Change doesn't require perfection—it requires participation.**

---

5. Turning Daily Actions into a Lifelong Commitment

□ *Real change happens when everyday actions become habits, not just one-time efforts.*

□ **How to Stay Committed to Change**

✓ **Set Small, Achievable Goals** – Focus on one action at a time (e.g., switching banks, reducing waste, joining a local group).

✓ **Find Like-Minded People** – Surround yourself with others who share your values.

✓ **Educate Yourself Continuously** – Stay informed about the issues you care about.

✓ **Teach & Inspire Others** – Help family and friends see the impact of their choices.

□ **Lesson: Activism is not an event—it's a way of life.**

Final Thought: You Are More Powerful Than You Think

□ **The system survives when people believe their actions don't matter.**

□ **But small, everyday choices are what fuel revolutions, shift economies, and transform societies.**

□ **You don't need permission, wealth, or a platform—you just need to start.**

The question is not whether small actions can change the world—the question is, will you take the first step? □

CHAPTER 33: HOW CHOOSING WHERE TO SHOP, WHAT TO WATCH, AND WHO TO SUPPORT INFLUENCES THE WORLD

"Every dollar you spend, every view you give, and every cause you support is a vote for the kind of world you want to live in."

Many people believe that change only happens through protests, elections, or laws, but the reality is that everyday decisions shape the world just as much. The choices we make—where we spend our money, what media we consume, and who we uplift—either reinforce the status quo or create pressure for change.

This chapter explores **how consumer choices, entertainment habits, and public support shape industries, influence policies, and force corporations to change.**

---

1. The Power of Consumer Choices: Where You Shop Matters

☐ *Every time you buy something, you are supporting a company's values, labor practices, and impact on society.*

☐ **How Your Purchases Shape the Economy**

☐ **Supporting Ethical Businesses Grows Sustainable Alternatives** – Local shops, worker-owned co-ops, and fair-trade brands invest in workers, not just profits.

☐ **Boycotting Exploitative Companies Forces Reform** – Companies change when they lose customers due to unethical behavior.

☐ **Investing in Community Strengthens Local Economies** – Shopping at small businesses keeps wealth circulating in the community.

☐ **Example: The Power of Boycotts**

☐ **Montgomery Bus Boycott (1955-1956)** – A year-long consumer strike forced the U.S. government to desegregate public transportation.

☐ **Nestlé Boycotts (1970s-Present)** – Consumer activism exposed Nestlé's unethical baby formula marketing in developing countries.

☐ **Nike & Sweatshop Protests (1990s-2000s)** – Public backlash over labor abuses forced Nike to improve factory conditions.

☐ **Lesson: Where you spend money either strengthens or weakens exploitative corporations.**

---

2. The Impact of Media Choices: What You Watch Shapes Culture

☐ *The media we consume influences our beliefs, social norms, and what industries succeed.*

☐ **How Entertainment Reinforces or Challenges the Status Quo**

☐ **Streaming & TV Choices Influence What Gets Produced** – Every view supports specific narratives, creators, and industries.

☐ **Movies & Shows Shape Social Attitudes** – Representation in media affects how people see race, gender, and political issues.

☐ **News Consumption Controls What People Believe** – Choosing independent journalism over corporate media prevents misinformation.

☐ **Example: When Media Changes Minds**

☐ **The Cosby Show (1980s)** – Changed public perception of Black families and contributed to social progress.

☐ **Blackfish (2013)** – A single documentary about SeaWorld's treatment of whales led to massive protests and policy changes.

☐ **#OscarsSoWhite (2015-2016)** – Online pressure forced Hollywood to diversify its casting and awards process.

☐ **Lesson: What you watch determines what industries prioritize—support media that educates, challenges, and inspires.**

---

3. Who You Support: The Influence of Public Figures & Movements

☐ *Who we amplify—whether politicians, activists, or celebrities—affects public discourse and policy decisions.*

☐ **How Public Support Creates Change**

☐ **Backing Independent Candidates Weakens Corrupt Political Systems** – Voting for grassroots leaders shifts government priorities.

☐ **Supporting Ethical Influencers & Creators Shifts Power Away from Corporations** – Independent media offers alternatives to corporate news.

☐ **Public Pressure Can Hold Leaders Accountable** – When mass support turns against unethical figures, they lose power.

Example: Public Pressure Changing Power

Colin Kaepernick (2016-Present) – Athlete-turned-activist lost his NFL career for kneeling during the anthem but became a global symbol of protest.

Harvey Weinstein & #MeToo (2017-Present) – Public exposure of Hollywood's abuse led to criminal trials and policy changes.

Greta Thunberg & Climate Action (2018-Present) – A single student protest sparked global youth-led climate movements.

Lesson: Who you support—or refuse to support—shapes political, cultural, and economic power structures.

---

4. Ethical Shopping: How to Align Spending with Your Values

If you wouldn't support an unethical politician, why support an unethical corporation?

How to Shop with a Conscience

✓ **Research Brands Before Buying** – Use sites like Ethical Consumer or Good On You to check corporate practices.
✓ **Buy Local & Fair Trade** – Choose small businesses and ethical supply chains over mass-produced goods.
✓ **Reduce Waste & Fast Fashion Consumption** – Avoid companies that exploit labor and harm the environment.
✓ **Use Sustainable Banking** – Bank with institutions that invest in communities, not oil or arms industries.

Lesson: Every purchase either funds oppression or supports ethical change—choose wisely.

---

5. The Internet as a Tool for Amplifying Ethical Choices

Online communities make it easier than ever to spread ethical choices and hold industries accountable.

How Digital Activism Magnifies Consumer Power

Social Media Boycotts Pressure Companies – Viral hashtags can force corporations to respond.

◻ **Review Bombing Exposes Corruption** – Bad press from online reviews hurts unethical brands.

◻ **Influencer Activism Shapes Consumer Trends** – Ethical influencers educate people on better choices.

◻ **Crowdsourced Watchlists Track Unethical Companies** – Online platforms keep corporations accountable.

◻ **Example: Social Media-Driven Change**

◻ **#DeleteUber (2017)** – A boycott over unethical business practices cost Uber millions in lost revenue.

◻ **Fashion Revolution (#WhoMadeMyClothes, 2013-Present)** – Exposed fast fashion's labor abuses, pressuring companies to improve transparency.

◻ **#StopHateForProfit (2020)** – Major brands pulled ads from Facebook due to its handling of hate speech.

◻ **Lesson: Digital communities give consumers collective power—when enough people withdraw support, industries are forced to change.**

---

6. Making Ethical Choices a Daily Habit

◻ *It's impossible to be perfect, but small, consistent actions add up.*

◻ **How to Maintain Long-Term Commitment**

✓ **Choose One Category to Focus On** – Whether it's ethical food, clothing, banking, or media, start somewhere.

✓ **Educate Friends & Family** – Share knowledge about why these choices matter.

✓ **Set Personal Guidelines** – For example, only buy from companies with ethical labor policies.

✓ **Remember That Every Choice Counts** – Even small changes, like switching a single product, create ripples.

◻ **Lesson: Sustainability in activism is about consistency, not perfection.**

Final Thought: You Are Always Voting With Your Choices

☐ Where you shop, what you watch, and who you support are not just personal choices—they are political and economic statements.

☐ Every dollar spent, every show streamed, and every public figure supported either strengthens or weakens exploitative systems.

☐ The system only has power because people keep fueling it— what happens when enough people stop?

The question is not whether your choices matter—the question is, are you making them consciously? ☐

CHAPTER 34: THE ROLE OF SMALL BUSINESSES AND LOCAL INITIATIVES IN RECLAIMING POWER

"When you buy from a small business, you're not just making a purchase—you're making a difference."

For decades, corporations and monopolies have dominated economies, draining wealth from communities while increasing profits for the ultra-rich. However, small businesses and local initiatives are the foundation of strong, independent economies that empower ordinary citizens. By shifting economic power from global corporations to local communities, small businesses help build resilience, create fair jobs, and keep wealth circulating where it belongs.

This chapter explores **how small businesses and local initiatives serve as an antidote to corporate exploitation and why supporting them is a revolutionary act.**

1. Why Small Businesses Matter

☐ *A strong economy is not one controlled by a few mega-corporations —it is one where wealth is spread among communities.*

☐ The Hidden Power of Small Businesses

☐ **Keep Wealth in Local Communities** – Every dollar spent locally generates more jobs and economic activity.

☐ **Reduce Corporate Monopoly Power** – Small businesses create competition and prevent industry control by a few mega-corporations.

☐ **Encourage Fair Wages & Better Working Conditions** – Unlike large corporations, local businesses often pay better wages and treat employees fairly.

☐ **Increase Community Self-Sufficiency** – When small businesses thrive, communities depend less on outside investors and corporations.

☐ Example: The Small Business Impact on Local Economies

☐ **For every $100 spent at a local business, $68 stays in the community**, compared to only $43 when spent at a corporate chain.

☐ **Small businesses employ nearly half of the workforce in most economies**, creating jobs and stability.

☐ **Communities with strong local businesses have lower poverty rates and higher civic engagement.**

☐ **Lesson: Small businesses decentralize economic power and prevent corporate control over our daily lives.**

2. The Dangers of Corporate Domination

☐ *When corporations replace small businesses, communities lose economic independence and become financially dependent on billionaires.*

☐ How Large Corporations Harm Local Economies

☐ **Monopolization:** Big companies crush local businesses, leaving fewer options for consumers and workers.

☐ **Low Wages & Exploitation:** Corporations prioritize profits over workers, offering unfair wages and poor working conditions.

☐ **Tax Avoidance:** Large corporations use loopholes to avoid paying taxes, shifting the burden to ordinary citizens.

☐ **Economic Drain:** Profits from corporate chains leave communities instead of being reinvested locally.

☐ **Example: The Walmart Effect**

☐ **When Walmart enters a town, local businesses often shut down, leading to job losses.**

☐ **Walmart workers are often underpaid, forcing them to rely on government assistance.**

☐ **The company profits billions while communities suffer from economic stagnation.**

☐ **Lesson: Corporate dominance is designed to extract wealth from local communities and transfer it to the elite.**

---

3. How Local Initiatives Strengthen Communities

☐ *True economic power doesn't come from billionaires—it comes from communities supporting each other.*

☐ **The Benefits of Local Initiatives**

☐ **Community-Owned Businesses Keep Power in the Hands of the People** – Worker-owned cooperatives ensure employees share in the profits.

☐ **Local Food Movements Reduce Dependence on Industrial Agriculture** – Farmers' markets and co-ops support sustainable agriculture.

☐ **Neighborhood-Based Services Provide Accessible & Fair Resources** – Local banking, healthcare, and education initiatives create stability.

☐ **Mutual Aid Networks Build Social & Economic Safety Nets** – Community members support one another without corporate involvement.

◻ **Example: Worker Cooperatives as Economic Resistance**

◻ **Mondragón (Spain):** A worker-owned cooperative that employs over 80,000 people with fair wages and benefits.

◻ **Cooperative Jackson (U.S.):** A Black-led economic initiative creating local jobs and community wealth.

◻ **New York City's Local Food Co-ops:** Empower small farmers and provide communities with fresh, ethical food.

◻ **Lesson: When people take control of their local economy, they reduce reliance on exploitative corporations.**

---

4. Supporting Small Businesses is an Act of Resistance

◻ *Where you spend your money determines whether you support local economies or strengthen corporate monopolies.*

◻ **How to Shift Power to Small Businesses**

✓ **Buy Local Instead of Supporting Chains** – Choose independent bookstores, coffee shops, and restaurants over large corporations.

✓ **Invest in Community-Owned Businesses** – Support cooperatives, small farms, and worker-led enterprises.

✓ **Use Credit Unions Instead of Big Banks** – Keep your money in financial institutions that invest in communities.

✓ **Encourage Entrepreneurship** – Help small business owners grow by spreading awareness and offering support.

◻ **Example: The Buy Local Movement**

◻ **"Small Business Saturday" was created to challenge Black Friday and encourage community spending.**

◻ **Cities that promote local businesses experience faster economic recovery and lower unemployment rates.**

◻ **Independent bookstores that were once in decline are now thriving due to consumer activism against Amazon.**

◻ **Lesson: Shifting even a small portion of spending toward local businesses has a massive economic impact.**

---

5. How Governments & Policies Can Support Small Businesses

While individuals play a role in supporting small businesses, governments must also create policies that protect them from corporate exploitation.

What Governments Can Do to Support Local Businesses

Close Tax Loopholes for Corporations – Level the playing field so small businesses can compete fairly.

Invest in Local Economic Development – Provide grants, low-interest loans, and training for small businesses.

Strengthen Antitrust Laws – Prevent corporate monopolies from crushing competition.

Simplify Regulations for Small Businesses – Reduce bureaucratic barriers that only large corporations can afford to navigate.

Example: How Policy Protects Small Businesses

Germany's strict laws against monopolies have helped small businesses thrive.

France's protections for independent bookstores prevent Amazon from undercutting prices unfairly.

Some U.S. cities have passed "formula business restrictions" to prevent chain stores from dominating local markets.

Lesson: Laws that protect small businesses lead to stronger economies, more jobs, and less corporate control.

---

6. Taking Action: How You Can Support Local Businesses

You don't need to start a business to strengthen your local economy —small everyday actions make a difference.

Steps to Support Small Businesses & Local Initiatives

✓ **Shift Your Spending Habits:** Choose small businesses whenever possible.

✓ **Promote Local Entrepreneurs:** Share their products and services on social media.

✓ **Participate in Community Initiatives:** Join local farmer's markets, co-ops, and neighborhood support groups.

✓ **Advocate for Small Business Protections:** Contact policymakers to demand fair laws.

✓ **Encourage Business Ownership:** If you have skills, consider starting your own small business or cooperative.

 Lesson: Building economic independence starts with daily choices—supporting small businesses is one of the easiest ways to fight corporate control.

Final Thought: Local Economies Create Real Freedom

 Big corporations want people to believe that supporting them is inevitable—it's not.

 Small businesses and local initiatives are the key to reclaiming economic power from monopolies.

 Every dollar spent at a small business strengthens a community and weakens corporate domination.

The question is not whether small businesses can challenge corporate power—the question is, will you help make it happen?

CHAPTER 35:
CASE STUDIES:
INDIVIDUALS WHO
MADE A DIFFERENCE
THROUGH SIMPLE
ACTIONS

"Never doubt that a small group of thoughtful, committed citizens can change the world. Indeed, it's the only thing that ever has." — Margaret Mead

Many people believe that only politicians, billionaires, or celebrities can create real change, but history proves otherwise. Some of the world's most powerful movements began with ordinary individuals taking small but courageous actions.

This chapter highlights **real people who changed the world— not through wealth or power, but through everyday choices**

that inspired massive change.

1. Rosa Parks: The Power of Saying "No"

□ *One act of defiance against injustice sparked a nationwide movement.*

□ What Happened?

□ In 1955, Rosa Parks, a Black woman in Montgomery, Alabama, **refused to give up her bus seat** to a white passenger.

□ She was arrested, but her simple act of resistance **ignited the Montgomery Bus Boycott**—one of the most important events in the U.S. Civil Rights Movement.

□ Thousands of Black citizens stopped using buses for over a year, **financially pressuring the city** to desegregate public transportation.

□ The Impact

□ **The boycott lasted 381 days** and cost the transit system huge financial losses.

□ **In 1956, the U.S. Supreme Court ruled that bus segregation was unconstitutional.**

□ **Rosa Parks became a global symbol of resistance, proving that even a single, simple action can spark a revolution.**

□ **Lesson: You don't need a megaphone or a political office to create change—sometimes, all it takes is saying "No."**

2. Greta Thunberg: A School Strike That Inspired the World

□ *One teenager skipping school to protest climate inaction grew into a global movement.*

□ What Happened?

□ In 2018, Greta Thunberg, a 15-year-old Swedish student, **started skipping school every Friday** to protest outside the Swedish parliament.

□ She held a sign saying **"School Strike for Climate"** and demanded stronger action against climate change.

◻ Her solo protest inspired millions of students worldwide to **join the Fridays for Future movement.**

◻ **The Impact**

◻ **Over 4 million people joined climate strikes in 2019,** making it one of the largest environmental protests in history.

◻ **Governments were forced to address climate policies,** with some countries declaring climate emergencies.

◻ **Thunberg spoke at the United Nations and directly challenged world leaders** for their inaction.

◻ **Lesson: One small, consistent action—like skipping school for a cause—can mobilize millions.**

---

3. Mohamed Bouazizi: A Fruit Vendor Who Sparked a Revolution

◻ *An act of desperation led to the fall of governments and changed the course of history.*

◻ **What Happened?**

◻ Mohamed Bouazizi was a poor street vendor in Tunisia who **struggled daily against police harassment and corruption.**

◻ In December 2010, after being **humiliated by authorities and having his goods confiscated,** he set himself on fire in protest.

◻ His death **sparked mass protests across Tunisia,** leading to the fall of the government and inspiring the Arab Spring—pro-democracy uprisings across the Middle East.

◻ **The Impact**

◻ **The Tunisian president was forced to step down, ending decades of dictatorship.**

◻ **The Arab Spring spread to Egypt, Libya, Syria, and beyond, leading to major political shifts.**

◻ **Millions of people found the courage to challenge oppressive regimes.**

◻ **Lesson: Even an individual act of resistance can ignite global change—but it should never come to this. Societies must listen** before desperation turns into revolution.

---

4. Malala Yousafzai: A Girl Who Defied the Taliban

Speaking up for education nearly cost her life—but it changed the world.

What Happened?

Malala Yousafzai was a young girl in Pakistan who loved going to school.

When the Taliban took over her town, **they banned girls from attending school.**

Malala **spoke out publicly, writing blogs and giving speeches** defending girls' right to education.

In 2012, **she was shot in the head by the Taliban**—but survived.

The Impact

Her survival and bravery inspired worldwide support for girls' education.

She became the youngest-ever Nobel Peace Prize winner in 2014.

Her foundation now helps educate millions of girls worldwide.

Lesson: Courageous voices—even from the youngest among us—can break oppressive silence.

---

5. Boyan Slat: A College Dropout Cleaning the Oceans

One engineering student turned an idea into the largest ocean cleanup project in history.

What Happened?

At age 16, Boyan Slat saw the devastating impact of plastic pollution in the ocean.

Instead of waiting for governments to act, he developed a system to **remove plastic waste from the ocean using natural currents.**

He dropped out of college to launch **The Ocean Cleanup**, which has now removed thousands of tons of plastic from the sea.

The Impact

His system is the first large-scale effort to clean the Great Pacific Garbage Patch.

Governments and companies have since pledged millions toward ocean cleanup.

His work proves that innovation, not just activism, can create environmental change.

Lesson: You don't need to be a scientist or billionaire to fix global problems—just someone willing to take action.

---

6. Julia "Butterfly" Hill: Saving a Forest by Living in a Tree

One woman spent over two years in a tree to stop deforestation.

What Happened?

In 1997, Julia Butterfly Hill climbed into a 1,500-year-old redwood tree in California to **stop logging companies from cutting it down.**

She lived **in the tree for 738 days**, enduring extreme weather, isolation, and harassment.

Her protest gained international media attention, forcing logging companies to **protect parts of the forest.**

The Impact

The tree (nicknamed "Luna") was permanently preserved.

Her actions helped fuel the global environmental movement.

She proved that personal sacrifice can inspire collective environmental consciousness.

Lesson: Defending the planet sometimes requires extreme dedication—but it works.

---

7. Jadav Payeng: The Man Who Planted a Forest

One man spent 40 years planting trees—and built a forest larger than Central Park.

☐ What Happened?

☐ In the 1970s, Jadav Payeng, an Indian farmer, noticed that erosion was destroying land near his village.

☐ He decided to **plant trees every single day** to restore the ecosystem.

☐ Over 40 years, he planted **over 1,400 acres of forest**—home to elephants, tigers, and rare birds.

☐ The Impact

☐ **He single-handedly restored an entire ecosystem.**

☐ **His work is now recognized as a global environmental success story.**

☐ **It proves that individual persistence can rebuild nature.**

☐ **Lesson: One person, one tree at a time, can change the planet.**

Final Thought: One Small Act Can Change the World

☐ **None of these individuals set out to change history—they just acted on what they believed was right.**

☐ **Small actions, repeated consistently, can challenge corrupt systems, inspire millions, and force powerful institutions to change.**

☐ **The system survives because people believe they are powerless—but history proves otherwise.**

The question is not whether you can make a difference—the question is, will you? ☐

CHAPTER 36: THE FUTURE OF THE ORDINARY CITIZEN

"The most powerful force for change is not politicians, corporations, or governments—it is ordinary people who refuse to accept the status quo."

T he future belongs not to the wealthiest or most powerful, but to those who understand their power as citizens, consumers, and members of society. Technology, political shifts, and economic systems are changing rapidly, and the ordinary citizen must adapt, reclaim control, and actively shape the future rather than passively accepting it.

This chapter explores **the challenges and opportunities ahead for ordinary citizens, the threats posed by corporate and governmental overreach, and the ways people can build a future where power is decentralized and justice is accessible to all.**

---

1. The New Challenges Facing Ordinary Citizens

 As power structures evolve, so do the ways in which ordinary people are controlled or manipulated.

▢ Key Threats to Citizen Power

▢ **Corporate Monopoly & Economic Control** – Fewer corporations control the global economy, limiting choices and financial independence.

▢ **Digital Surveillance & Privacy Erosion** – Governments and tech giants track, manipulate, and influence citizens more than ever.

▢ **Misinformation & Propaganda Warfare** – The battle for truth is becoming harder as fake news and deepfakes spread.

▢ **Political Polarization & Division** – Citizens are divided by ideology, making it harder to unite for common causes.

▢ **Climate Crisis & Resource Scarcity** – Ordinary people will bear the brunt of environmental destruction while corporations profit.

▢ **Lesson: The future will be defined by whether citizens passively accept these challenges or actively fight back.**

---

2. The Role of Technology: A Tool for Liberation or Oppression?

▢ *Technology can either empower people or enslave them—it all depends on who controls it.*

▢ How Technology is Used Against Citizens

▢ **Mass Surveillance:** Governments and corporations monitor online activity, limiting freedom of speech.

▢ **Algorithmic Control:** Social media manipulates emotions, influences elections, and deepens division.

▢ **Automation & Job Loss:** AI and robotics threaten millions of jobs, concentrating wealth at the top.

▢ How Citizens Can Use Technology for Liberation

▢ **Decentralized Platforms:** Use encrypted messaging, blockchain voting, and open-source tools to bypass centralized control.

 Digital Activism: Leverage social media to mobilize people, expose corruption, and share uncensored news.

 Skill Development: Learn AI, coding, digital security, and automation to stay ahead in a changing job market.

 Lesson: Technology is a double-edged sword—if citizens don't take control of it, those in power will use it against them.

---

3. The Future of Work: Breaking Free from Economic Dependence

 The traditional 9-to-5 job model is dying—citizens must adapt or be left behind.

 The Problem with Traditional Employment

 Wages Stagnate While Costs Rise: The gap between income and expenses continues to grow.

 Corporations Exploit Workers: Gig economy jobs (Uber, DoorDash) keep people in financial instability.

 Job Automation: AI and robots are replacing millions of human workers.

 How Citizens Can Build Economic Independence

 Entrepreneurship & Small Businesses: Creating your own source of income weakens corporate control.

 Remote Work & Digital Skills: Learning high-income digital skills (coding, marketing, consulting) creates new opportunities.

 Worker Cooperatives & Shared Ownership: Businesses owned by employees prevent corporate exploitation.

 Lesson: The future belongs to those who create their own economic freedom—not those who wait for corporations to provide it.

---

4. The Shift Toward Decentralized Power

 Centralized power benefits the elite—decentralization empowers ordinary citizens.

What is Decentralization?

Decentralized Finance (DeFi): Cryptocurrencies and blockchain reduce reliance on banks.

Decentralized Social Media: Platforms like Mastodon, Minds, and blockchain-based apps prevent corporate censorship.

Community-Based Governance: Local decision-making reduces reliance on corrupt national governments.

The Power of Local Action

Small businesses, local agriculture, and community initiatives make people less dependent on large institutions.

Decentralized finance allows individuals to control their own wealth rather than relying on corrupt banking systems.

Digital privacy tools protect individuals from surveillance and exploitation.

Lesson: The more power is decentralized, the harder it is for governments and corporations to control people.

---

5. Reclaiming Political Power as a Citizen

Political systems are designed to make ordinary citizens feel powerless—this is a lie.

How the System Tricks People into Apathy

Voting Suppression & Rigged Systems: Many feel their votes don't matter because the system is designed to maintain elite control.

Media Manipulation: News corporations distort reality to benefit political and economic elites.

Disillusionment & Division: Political parties use culture wars to distract from economic and systemic corruption.

How Citizens Can Reclaim Political Power

Local Elections Matter: City councils, school boards, and district attorneys shape daily life more than national politics.

Direct Action Works: Strikes, protests, and mass movements force politicians to listen.

- **Alternative Governance Models:** Participatory democracy, blockchain voting, and grassroots organizing challenge corrupt systems.

- **Lesson: Ordinary people hold more political power than they think—but only if they use it.**

---

6. Building a Future Where Citizens Thrive

- *The future can either be dictated by corporations and governments, or shaped by active citizens—what happens next depends on us.*

- **What a Citizen-Driven Future Looks Like**

- **Economic Freedom:** People own businesses, control their wealth, and are not dependent on corporations.
- **Digital Privacy & Decentralization:** Citizens control their own information and communication.
- **Sustainable Communities:** Local economies, ethical production, and eco-friendly policies ensure long-term survival.
- **Stronger Civic Engagement:** People are informed, involved, and directly influence policies affecting their lives.

- **How to Start Creating That Future**

✓ **Take Ownership of Your Finances** – Stop relying on corporate jobs and build multiple income streams.
✓ **Use Technology for Freedom, Not Control** – Learn digital privacy, blockchain, and decentralized platforms.
✓ **Engage in Your Local Community** – The strongest resistance to centralized control starts at the local level.
✓ **Educate Others & Build Networks** – Share knowledge, mentor others, and create activist communities.

- **Lesson: The future isn't something we wait for—it's something we create.**

Final Thought: The Future Belongs to the People Who Take Action

☐ The future of the ordinary citizen depends on whether people accept control or fight for independence.

☐ Technology, economics, and politics are evolving rapidly—either people shape these changes, or they become victims of them.

☐ The system is designed to make citizens feel small, but history proves that real power has always belonged to the people.

The question is not whether ordinary citizens have power—the question is, will you use it? ☐

CHAPTER 37: PREDICTIONS: HOW TECHNOLOGY WILL FURTHER EMPOWER THE INDIVIDUAL

"The same technology that can be used to control people can also be used to set them free."

Technology has always been a double-edged sword—it can be a tool for liberation or a mechanism for control. While corporations and governments use technology for surveillance, censorship, and economic domination, ordinary citizens can harness it for empowerment, independence, and resistance.

This chapter explores **how future technological advancements will further empower individuals**, offering them greater control over their finances, privacy, knowledge, and governance.

1. Decentralized Finance (DeFi): Financial Freedom from Banks

& Governments

The future of finance is one where individuals control their own money—without banks or corrupt institutions.

How DeFi Will Empower Ordinary Citizens

Freedom from Bank Control – People can store, send, and receive money without relying on centralized banks.

No More Banking Fees & Middlemen – Peer-to-peer transactions cut out exploitative financial institutions.

Access to Global Markets – People in developing countries can participate in global economies without restrictions.

Protection from Inflation & Economic Crises – Cryptocurrencies and stablecoins offer alternatives when national currencies collapse.

Example: Bitcoin & Cryptocurrencies

In Venezuela, citizens turned to Bitcoin when their national currency collapsed.

Remittances using crypto are faster and cheaper than bank transfers, especially in corrupt or unstable regions.

Governments are trying to regulate or ban crypto—because they fear losing financial control over citizens.

Prediction: By 2030, digital currencies will become the primary means of financial transactions for millions, weakening the influence of traditional banks.

---

2. Privacy & Encryption: Taking Back Control of Personal Data

As surveillance increases, so will tools that allow citizens to protect their digital lives.

The Future of Digital Privacy

End-to-End Encrypted Messaging – Apps like Signal and decentralized communication networks will make surveillance harder.

Decentralized Social Media – Platforms that are not controlled by corporations (like Mastodon) will replace Facebook & Twitter.

▢ **Blockchain-Based Identity Systems** – Digital identities will be controlled by individuals, not governments.

▢ **Personal AI Assistants for Privacy** – AI tools will automatically detect and block digital tracking and targeted manipulation.

▢ **Example: Rise of Privacy-Focused Tools**

▢ **DuckDuckGo is growing as an alternative to Google, offering tracking-free search.**

▢ **Tor and VPNs are increasingly used to bypass censorship and protect anonymity.**

▢ **Governments in China and the U.S. are trying to weaken encryption because it gives people too much control.**

▢ **Prediction: By 2025, privacy-focused technology will become mainstream, with people prioritizing security over convenience.**

---

3. AI & Automation: Replacing Work, But Also Creating New Opportunities

▢ *Artificial intelligence is disrupting industries, eliminating jobs—but also opening new pathways to financial independence.*

▢ **How AI Will Empower Individuals**

▢ **AI-Powered Education & Skill Building** – Free, AI-driven education will allow anyone to learn high-income skills.

▢ **Automation of Repetitive Work** – People will have more freedom to pursue creative and meaningful work.

▢ **AI Assistants for Activism & Business** – Individuals will use AI to automate advocacy, marketing, and content creation.

▢ **New Digital Economy Opportunities** – AI will help people build businesses without needing large teams.

▢ **Example: AI for Economic Empowerment**

▢ **ChatGPT & AI tools are already enabling freelancers, writers, and programmers to earn more with less effort.**

▢ **AI-generated content is challenging traditional media**

THE POWER OF THE ORDINARY CITIZEN

control over narratives.

 As AI improves, it will democratize knowledge, making expertise available to all.

 Prediction: By 2035, AI will allow individuals to generate passive income, automate businesses, and reduce reliance on traditional jobs.

---

4. Decentralized Governance: The Future of Democracy

 Technology will shift power away from centralized governments and toward direct citizen participation.

 How Technology Will Change Governance

 Blockchain-Based Voting – Eliminates fraud and corruption in elections.

 Smart Contracts for Government Services – Removes bureaucracy and inefficiency by automating processes.

 Digital Direct Democracy – Citizens vote on laws and policies directly instead of relying on politicians.

 Global Citizenship & Stateless Societies – People will choose decentralized governance models, rather than being tied to nation-states.

 Example: Experiments in Digital Governance

 Estonia has implemented blockchain voting and digital citizenship, making government processes more transparent.

 Decentralized autonomous organizations (DAOs) allow people to manage communities and businesses without central leadership.

 The more corrupt a government is, the more it resists these innovations—because they weaken state control.

 Prediction: By 2040, many traditional governments will be replaced by decentralized, community-driven governance systems.

---

5. The Metaverse & Digital Societies: A New Frontier for

Activism & Economic Power

The metaverse will be more than just entertainment—it will be a new space for activism, education, and economic independence.

How the Metaverse Will Empower People

Decentralized Virtual Economies – People will earn, trade, and interact in digital economies independent of nation-states.

Global Collaboration for Activism – Activists will organize and protest in virtual spaces that authoritarian governments cannot control.

Education Without Borders – Schools, universities, and skill training will happen in virtual reality, making knowledge accessible to all.

Ownership of Digital Assets – People will control their own data, art, and businesses through NFTs and blockchain.

Example: How Virtual Reality is Already Changing the World

People are attending virtual protests in the metaverse to bypass real-world restrictions.

Cryptocurrency is being used as a financial escape route for people in oppressive regimes.

Online gaming communities are creating new economies, where players can earn real money.

Prediction: By 2045, digital societies will rival physical nations in economic and political influence.

---

6. Education & Self-Learning: The Rise of the Independent Thinker

The future of education is not in schools—it is in the hands of individuals who take learning into their own control.

How Education Will Be Transformed

AI Tutors & Personalized Learning – Individuals will learn faster and better with AI-driven programs.

Decentralized Knowledge Networks – Open-source, peer-to-peer learning will replace traditional universities.

THE POWER OF THE ORDINARY CITIZEN

 Gamified Education & Skill Building – People will learn through interactive experiences, making education more engaging.

 No More Gatekeepers to Information – Anyone with internet access can become an expert without needing a degree.

 Example: The Death of Traditional Schooling

 Homeschooling and online education are rising globally, challenging government-mandated curriculums.

 Independent thinkers are rejecting traditional universities in favor of self-learning.

 More people are questioning institutional education as a tool for control rather than enlightenment.

 Prediction: By 2050, traditional education systems will collapse in favor of decentralized, self-directed learning.

Final Thought: The Future Belongs to Those Who Adapt & Take Control

 Technology will either empower individuals or enslave them —how it is used depends on who controls it.

 Ordinary citizens who embrace decentralization, privacy, and digital independence will thrive.

 The system fears an informed, technologically empowered population—because that is how real change happens.

The question is not whether technology will change the world —the question is, will you use it to claim your freedom?

CHAPTER 38: WHAT THE WORLD WOULD LOOK LIKE IF MORE CITIZENS EMBRACED THEIR POWER

"A society of empowered citizens is a society where governments serve the people, not control them."

The world we live in today is shaped by passivity, corporate greed, and government overreach. But what if more people recognized their power and actively worked to reshape society? What if ordinary citizens reclaimed control over economics, politics, technology, and their communities? This chapter explores **a vision of a world where individuals fully embrace their power, challenge the status quo, and build a future where freedom, fairness, and opportunity thrive.**

1. The End of Corporate Domination: A Fair Economy for All

☐ *If citizens reclaimed their financial power, corporations would lose their ability to exploit workers and consumers.*

☐ What This World Would Look Like

☐ **Small Businesses & Cooperatives Would Replace Monopolies** – Instead of massive corporations, worker-owned businesses would thrive.

☐ **Local Economies Would Be Stronger** – Communities would circulate their wealth locally, reducing reliance on global corporations.

☐ **Fair Wages & Worker Rights Would Be Universal** – People would demand and enforce better working conditions.

☐ **No More Debt Traps** – Citizens would prioritize economic independence, using decentralized finance instead of predatory banks.

☐ Example: If More People Boycotted Unethical Corporations

☐ **Amazon's exploitative labor practices would collapse if enough people stopped using its services.**

☐ **Walmart would be forced to pay fair wages if customers shifted to local businesses.**

☐ **Big banks would lose power if more citizens moved to credit unions and decentralized finance.**

☐ **Reality Check: Corporations only exist because people feed them—if citizens shift their financial habits, they can break the monopoly system.**

---

2. A Truly Democratic Society: People, Not Politicians, in Control

☐ *If citizens reclaimed their political power, governments would be forced to serve the people—not the elites.*

☐ What This World Would Look Like

☐ **Direct Democracy Would Replace Corrupt Political Systems** – Citizens would vote directly on policies rather than relying on politicians.

◻ **Community Governance Would Replace Top-Down Control** – Local people would manage resources and policies instead of bureaucrats.

◻ **Politicians Would Be Held Accountable** – Governments would no longer be able to ignore the will of the people.

◻ **Corruption Would Be Exposed & Punished** – More transparency would eliminate backdoor deals between corporations and politicians.

◻ **Example: If More People Voted in Local Elections & Held Leaders Accountable**

◻ **Lobbying power would weaken because elected officials would be directly accountable to their communities.**

◻ **Corrupt leaders would have no choice but to resign or be removed.**

◻ **New policies would reflect the needs of ordinary citizens, not corporate donors.**

◻ **Reality Check: Governments maintain control because people feel powerless—but if enough people demand change, the system must comply.**

---

3. A Surveillance-Free, Decentralized Internet

◻ *If citizens controlled their own data and online spaces, digital freedom would be a reality instead of a privilege.*

◻ **What This World Would Look Like**

◻ **Decentralized Social Media Would Replace Corporate Platforms** – No more censorship, manipulation, or algorithmic control.

◻ **Personal Data Would Belong to Individuals, Not Companies** – People would control who accesses their information.

◻ **Government Censorship Would Be Impossible** – Information would be stored across independent, global networks.

◻ **Freedom of Speech Would Be Fully Protected** – No corporation or government would have the power to silence citizens.

□ Example: If More People Used Encrypted Communication & Decentralized Platforms

□ **Surveillance capitalism (Google, Facebook, Amazon)** would collapse if people stopped using their services.
□ **Governments would struggle to suppress dissent** if encrypted, peer-to-peer networks became the norm.
□ **Misinformation would be harder to spread** if people used open-source, transparent news sources.

□ **Reality Check: The internet was designed to be decentralized —citizens just need to reclaim it.**

---

4. A Self-Sustaining Society: No More Dependence on the System

□ *If more citizens embraced self-sufficiency, they would no longer be at the mercy of corporate supply chains and government policies.*

□ **What This World Would Look Like**

□ **Community-Owned Food Systems Would Replace Factory Farming** – No more reliance on industrial agriculture.
□ **Renewable Energy Would Be Citizen-Controlled** – Individuals and neighborhoods would produce their own power.
□ **People Would Learn Practical Skills Again** – Basic survival skills (gardening, carpentry, repair work) would be common knowledge.
□ **Cooperative Housing Would End Landlord Exploitation** – People would own their homes collectively instead of paying high rents to investors.

□ **Example: If More People Grew Their Own Food & Used Renewable Energy**

□ **Big agriculture corporations would lose their power** over food supply chains.
□ **Oil companies would collapse** if communities powered themselves.
□ More people would be able to live independently without

relying on exploitative employers.

☐ **Reality Check: A self-sufficient society is possible—the system just convinces people they need it.**

---

5. A Culture of Critical Thinking & Independent Thought

☐ *If citizens stopped accepting media narratives at face value and started questioning authority, society would shift dramatically.*

☐ **What This World Would Look Like**

☐ **People Would Recognize & Resist Propaganda** – Governments and corporations would struggle to control narratives.

☐ **Education Would Prioritize Critical Thinking, Not Memorization** – Schools would teach students how to analyze, not just obey.

☐ **Independent Media Would Replace Corporate News** – Citizens would fund and consume journalism that prioritizes truth, not profit.

☐ **Debates Would Be Fact-Based, Not Emotionally Manipulated** – Public discourse would shift from polarization to solutions.

☐ **Example: If More People Stopped Consuming Mainstream Media Uncritically**

☐ **News corporations would lose influence, forcing them to produce truthful content.**

☐ **Governments would struggle to manufacture consent for war, surveillance, and corruption.**

☐ **More people would engage in meaningful discussions instead of blindly following political tribes.**

☐ **Reality Check: A well-informed society is harder to control—education is the foundation of resistance.**

---

6. A Global Network of Empowered Citizens

☐ *If citizens worldwide connected, organized, and collaborated, no government or corporation could stop them.*

☐ **What This World Would Look Like**

 International Solidarity Movements Would Rise – People across borders would fight together against corruption and oppression.

 Whistleblowers Would Be Protected & Supported – Corrupt institutions would be exposed faster.

 Global Economic & Political Power Would Shift to the People – No single government or company could dominate society.

 Human Rights Would Be Enforced by the People, Not Politicians – Justice systems would be accountable to global citizens, not elites.

 Example: If More Citizens Used the Internet for Activism & Global Cooperation

 Protests and boycotts would be coordinated across countries, making them more effective.

 Grassroots funding for whistleblowers, independent media, and activists would challenge elite control.

 Dictators and corrupt leaders would face pressure not just from their citizens, but from a globally connected resistance.

 Reality Check: Globalization has given corporations more power—but it has also given citizens more power. It's time to use it.

Final Thought: A Society Where Citizens Rule Themselves

 If enough people embraced their power, governments would be forced to serve, not rule.

 Corporations would no longer be able to exploit workers, consumers, and communities.

 The internet would be a tool for liberation, not surveillance.

 Knowledge, wealth, and opportunities would belong to the many, not the few.

The question is not whether this world is possible—the question is, will you help build it?

CHAPTER 39: A CALL TO ACTION: HOW EVERY READER CAN START MAKING A DIFFERENCE TODAY

"The most powerful weapon in the world is an informed and active citizen."

Everything you have read so far proves one undeniable truth: the world is not shaped by governments, corporations, or billionaires—it is shaped by people who take action. Every revolution, every shift in history, every moment of progress started because ordinary citizens refused to accept the status quo.

But **change does not happen by accident**—it happens because people decide to act. **Now it's your turn.**

This final chapter outlines **simple, actionable steps that anyone—no matter where they are—can take today to start** reclaiming power, resisting exploitation, and creating a better future.

1. Shift Your Money: Stop Funding Your Oppressors

Every dollar you spend either strengthens or weakens exploitative systems.

Actions You Can Take Today

✓ **Support Small & Local Businesses** – Stop enriching corporations that exploit workers and communities.

✓ **Use Ethical Banking & Investments** – Move your money to credit unions, ethical funds, and decentralized finance.

✓ **Boycott Corrupt Corporations** – Avoid companies that engage in labor abuse, environmental destruction, or political manipulation.

✓ **Reduce Debt & Increase Financial Independence** – The less you owe, the less control banks and corporations have over you.

Impact: If millions of people shift their spending and banking habits, corporations will be forced to change or collapse.

2. Reclaim Your Political Power: Engage in the System & Hold Leaders Accountable

The system survives because people don't participate. Make them fear your involvement.

Actions You Can Take Today

✓ **Vote in Local Elections** – City councils, school boards, and district attorneys have direct impact on your life.

✓ **Contact Your Representatives** – Politicians ignore those who stay silent—demand action on key issues.

✓ **Push for Transparency & Accountability** – Support policies that expose corruption and prevent corporate influence.

✓ **Run for Office or Support Grassroots Candidates** – Real change comes from those who refuse to sell out.

 Impact: If more people engaged in local politics, corrupt officials would be removed, and policies would reflect real public needs.

---

3. Control Your Information: Stop Being Manipulated

 Media is the most powerful tool used to control people—take control of what you consume.

 Actions You Can Take Today

✓ **Fact-Check Everything** – Do not blindly trust news from corporate-owned media.

✓ **Support Independent Journalists** – Subscribe to investigative platforms instead of mainstream propaganda.

✓ **Encourage Critical Thinking in Your Community** – Teach others how to identify misinformation and bias.

✓ **Avoid Doomscrolling & Algorithmic Manipulation** – Take breaks from social media and seek out real discussions.

 Impact: A well-informed society is harder to manipulate—when enough people see through propaganda, governments and corporations lose control.

---

4. Strengthen Your Community: Build Local Power

 A strong local community is the best defense against corporate and governmental control.

 Actions You Can Take Today

✓ **Join or Start a Mutual Aid Group** – Help neighbors with food, housing, and support outside of government control.

✓ **Attend Local Meetings & Organize Events** – Build networks of engaged citizens to address real issues.

✓ **Create Alternative Economic Systems** – Bartering, co-ops, and local trade reduce reliance on exploitative systems.

✓ **Promote Community Self-Sufficiency** – Grow food, share resources, and teach survival skills.

 Impact: When communities rely on each other, they become

harder to exploit or control.

---

5. Use Technology for Liberation, Not Control

The digital world can either enslave you or set you free—choose wisely.

Actions You Can Take Today

✓ **Use Encrypted & Decentralized Platforms** – Switch to Signal, ProtonMail, and decentralized social media.
✓ **Protect Your Privacy** – Use VPNs, block tracking software, and avoid sharing excessive personal data.
✓ **Learn Digital Activism & Cybersecurity** – Know how to resist surveillance and censorship.
✓ **Help Others Escape Digital Exploitation** – Teach friends and family how to protect their data and privacy.

Impact: If more people controlled their own digital presence, corporations and governments would lose their grip on public discourse.

---

6. Take Ownership of Your Education & Skills

Knowledge is the foundation of independence—never let the system decide what you learn.

Actions You Can Take Today

✓ **Self-Educate & Develop Critical Thinking** – Read widely, question narratives, and seek alternative perspectives.
✓ **Learn Skills That Increase Independence** – Financial literacy, coding, survival skills, and creative problem-solving are essential.
✓ **Teach & Share Knowledge with Others** – Build a culture of learning within your community.
✓ **Challenge Institutionalized Education** – Push for real, meaningful education instead of indoctrination.

Impact: An informed population cannot be controlled—education is the ultimate tool of resistance.

7. Get Involved in Collective Action & Resistance

A single person can inspire change, but collective action forces it.

Actions You Can Take Today

✓ **Join or Support Protests & Strikes** – Mass movements create undeniable pressure for change.
✓ **Boycott & Divest from Corrupt Institutions** – Stop funding those who exploit and manipulate.
✓ **Use Social Media to Mobilize Others** – Share resources, educate, and amplify important issues.
✓ **Network with Like-Minded Activists** – Build alliances across movements to increase collective strength.

Impact: When enough people mobilize, governments and corporations are forced to listen.

8. Build a Long-Term Mindset for Change

Change doesn't happen overnight—persistence is the key to revolution.

How to Stay Committed

✓ **Set Realistic, Achievable Goals** – Start with one action and build from there.
✓ **Stay Informed, but Avoid Burnout** – Take breaks, but never disengage completely.
✓ **Encourage Others to Join the Movement** – The more people who act, the faster change happens.
✓ **Remember That Every Action Counts** – Even the smallest step contributes to something bigger.

Impact: Movements fail when people give up—sustained effort is what breaks oppressive systems.

Final Thought: Change Begins with You

You do not need permission to take back your power.
The system only thrives when people believe they are

powerless.

☐ Every dollar spent, every vote cast, every conversation had, and every act of defiance matters.

☐ History is shaped by those who take action—will you be one of them?

The question is not whether you can make a difference—the question is, will you start today? ☐

PART FIVE: YOU ARE MORE POWERFUL THAN YOU THINK

CHAPTER 40: KEY TAKEAWAYS: THE POWER OF THE ORDINARY CITIZEN

"The most powerful citizen is the one who understands their own strength."

This book has revealed a fundamental truth: ordinary people have always shaped history, economies, and societies. The system is designed to make you feel powerless—but the moment you realize the power you hold, everything changes.

Below are the key lessons from this journey:

1. The Illusion of Powerlessness is a Lie

▢ *The system thrives when people believe they have no control—but history proves otherwise.*

▢ **Every major movement—civil rights, workers' rights, climate action—began with ordinary people taking small** steps.

☐ **Corporations, politicians, and media work hard to manipulate and divide people because they fear united action.**

☐ **Your choices—how you vote, what you buy, what you believe —either reinforce or challenge the system.**

☐ **Lesson: You are not powerless. The system only succeeds when people fail to act.**

---

2. Small, Everyday Actions Create Massive Change

☐ *Change doesn't always come from revolutions—it happens through daily, intentional choices.*

☐ **Economic Power:** Where you spend your money determines which businesses and industries survive.

☐ **Political Power:** Local elections and grassroots activism have more impact than waiting for national change.

☐ **Cultural Influence:** What you watch, share, and promote shapes the future of media, education, and public discourse.

☐ **Community Engagement:** Strong local networks reduce dependence on corrupt systems and build real independence.

☐ **Lesson: Every purchase, vote, conversation, and action contributes to shaping the world around you.**

---

3. Corporations & Governments Need You More Than You Need Them

☐ *If citizens withdrew their support, corrupt institutions would collapse overnight.*

☐ **Monopolies exist because people keep feeding them— boycotts and consumer shifts force industries to change.**

☐ **Governments only stay in power if people comply —mass movements, protests, and civic engagement force accountability.**

☐ **Surveillance and media control exist because those in power know that an informed population is dangerous.**

◻ **Lesson:** Corporations and governments rely on your participation—choose wisely where you give your power.

---

4. The Digital Age is a Double-Edged Sword—Use it Wisely

◻ *Technology can be used for control or liberation—the choice is yours.*

◻ **Surveillance and censorship are growing, but encryption, VPNs, and decentralized platforms offer freedom.**
◻ **Social media can manipulate minds, but it can also be used to educate, organize, and mobilize.**
◻ **Artificial intelligence and automation will eliminate jobs, but they also create opportunities for financial independence.**

◻ **Lesson: Technology is not inherently good or bad—it depends on how citizens use it.**

---

5. The Future Belongs to Those Who Take Action

◻ *The difference between the world staying the same or becoming something better is whether people choose to act.*

◻ **Imagine a world where more people supported ethical businesses, voted in local elections, and educated themselves.**
◻ **Imagine communities that were self-sufficient, where citizens controlled their own resources, media, and governance.**
◻ **Imagine a society where people rejected corporate control, media propaganda, and political corruption.**

◻ **Lesson: The world will change only when enough people decide to change it.**

---

6. Your Next Steps: What You Can Do Right Now

◻ *No action is too small—every step matters.*

✓ **Shift Your Spending:** Support small businesses, ethical companies, and community banks.
✓ **Engage in Politics:** Vote, contact representatives, and hold

leaders accountable.

✓ **Control Your Digital Presence:** Use encryption, decentralized platforms, and independent media.

✓ **Strengthen Your Community:** Build local support networks, invest in self-sufficiency, and educate others.

✓ **Keep Learning & Questioning:** The more informed you are, the harder it is to be controlled.

 Lesson: If enough people take small actions consistently, the system will be forced to change.

Final Thought: You Are More Powerful Than You Think

 The system survives on compliance. The moment you stop blindly complying, you begin to reclaim your power.

 History proves that real change always starts with ordinary people who refuse to accept the status quo.

 The only thing standing between you and a better world is the belief that your actions don't matter.

The question is not whether you can make a difference—the question is, will you start today?

CHAPTER 41: A FINAL MOTIVATIONAL PUSH: HISTORY IS SHAPED BY THOSE WHO REFUSE TO REMAIN SILENT

"The world changes not because of those who complain, but because of those who refuse to accept things as they are."

History is not written by those who stay silent. It is written by those who speak up, those who take action, those who refuse to accept the status quo. Every right you have today—your freedom, your vote, your ability to speak openly—was fought for by people who decided that silence was not an option.

The future will be no different. **The world you leave behind will** be shaped by whether you choose to act or do nothing.

The question is simple: **Will you be a spectator or a participant in history?**

1. Every Major Change Began With Ordinary People Taking Action

☐ *The greatest revolutions in history were started not by politicians, but by ordinary people who refused to comply.*

☐ **The Civil Rights Movement succeeded because people risked everything to demand justice.**
☐ **Women's suffrage was won because millions refused to accept second-class citizenship.**
☐ **Workers' rights were secured because employees walked off their jobs, demanding fair wages and conditions.**
☐ **Corrupt governments have fallen because brave individuals refused to remain silent.**

☐ **Lesson: Every right you enjoy today exists because someone before you refused to stay quiet.**

2. The System Wants You to Feel Powerless—Because It Fears You

☐ *If ordinary citizens were truly powerless, governments and corporations wouldn't work so hard to control them.*

☐ **Why do authoritarian regimes censor free speech? Because words can ignite revolutions.**
☐ **Why do corporations manipulate consumers? Because informed people will stop buying into their lies.**
☐ **Why do elites rig systems to benefit themselves? Because if people united, the entire system would collapse.**

☐ **Lesson: The fact that they try so hard to control you is proof of how much power you actually have.**

3. You Don't Need Permission to Reclaim Your Power

▢ *Too many people wait for the "right moment" to act. The right moment is now.*

▢ **You don't need permission to stop funding corrupt corporations—just start buying from ethical businesses.**

▢ **You don't need permission to educate yourself—start reading, questioning, and thinking critically today.**

▢ **You don't need permission to hold leaders accountable—start voting, protesting, and demanding better policies now.**

▢ **You don't need permission to be a leader—every great movement started with one person deciding to act.**

▢ **Lesson: Change happens when people stop waiting and start doing.**

---

4. The Future Will Belong to Those Who Take Action

▢ *The world is being shaped right now. The only question is: who will shape it?*

▢ **Will corporations decide the future, or will people demand ethical economies?**

▢ **Will governments restrict freedoms, or will citizens fight for democracy?**

▢ **Will technology be used to control, or will people use it to liberate themselves?**

▢ **Will you live in a world shaped by others, or will you take part in shaping it?**

▢ **Lesson: If you do nothing, the future will be decided for you— by those who don't have your best interests at heart.**

---

5. The Final Challenge: Will You Be One of the Brave?

▢ *One hundred years from now, when people look back on this moment in history, what will they see?*

Will they see a generation that sat back and let injustice, corruption, and corporate greed shape the world?

Or will they see a generation that **took back its power, fought** for what was right, and built something better?

☐ History does not remember those who stayed silent. It remembers those who spoke up, stood up, and acted.

☐ The world is waiting. The revolution begins with you. Will you answer the call? ☐

CHAPTER 42: A ROADMAP FOR READERS TO BEGIN THEIR OWN JOURNEY OF IMPACT

"The journey of a thousand miles begins with a single step." — Lao Tzu

Now that you understand your power as an ordinary citizen, the next step is to turn knowledge into action. Change does not happen overnight, and no one can do everything at once—but everyone can do something.

This roadmap provides **clear, actionable steps** to help you begin your journey toward making a real impact in your community, your country, and the world.

Step 1: Identify Your Cause & Passion

☐ *You don't have to fix everything—but you can focus on one thing that matters most to you.*

▢ Questions to Ask Yourself

▢ What injustice or problem makes you the angriest?

▢ What issue do you feel most passionate about?

▢ What change do you wish you could see in your community or the world?

▢ Examples of Causes You Can Take Action On

✓ **Economic Justice** – Supporting small businesses, fighting corporate greed.

✓ **Political Reform** – Holding leaders accountable, engaging in activism.

✓ **Environmental Action** – Reducing waste, supporting sustainability.

✓ **Human Rights & Social Justice** – Fighting for equality, fair wages, and freedoms.

✓ **Digital Privacy & Free Speech** – Defending against censorship and surveillance.

▢ **Action Step: Choose one cause that deeply resonates with you and commit to learning more about it.**

Step 2: Educate Yourself & Question Everything

▢ *Knowledge is power—if you don't control your own information, someone else will control it for you.*

▢ How to Become an Informed Citizen

▢ **Read Books & Articles** – Challenge mainstream narratives and seek diverse perspectives.

▢ **Follow Independent Journalists** – Support investigative reporters who expose truth, not corporate interests.

▢ **Join Discussion Groups** – Engage in conversations that challenge and refine your thinking.

▢ **Question Authority** – Never accept government, corporate, or media statements at face value.

▢ **Action Step: Make a commitment to spend at least 15 minutes** a day learning about your chosen cause.

Step 3: Shift Your Economic Power

Money is one of the most powerful tools of influence—use it wisely.

How to Reclaim Financial Power

✓ **Boycott unethical corporations** – Research and avoid businesses that exploit workers and the environment.

✓ **Support small & local businesses** – Keep wealth circulating in your community.

✓ **Bank with ethical institutions** – Move money from big banks to credit unions or ethical fintech platforms.

✓ **Reduce personal debt & financial dependence** – The less you owe, the more freedom you have.

Action Step: Pick one major corporation to stop supporting and replace it with an ethical alternative.

Step 4: Take Political & Civic Action

Governments only listen to those who make their voices heard.

How to Get Involved Politically

Register & Vote in Local Elections – City councils and school boards impact daily life more than presidential elections.

Contact Your Representatives – Send emails, make calls, and demand change on issues that matter.

Join or Support Activist Movements – Get involved in protests, petitions, and policy advocacy.

Encourage Others to Participate – Help friends and family understand the importance of civic engagement.

Action Step: Find out when your next local election is and commit to voting.

Step 5: Build & Strengthen Your Community

A strong community is the best defense against corporate and government overreach.

☐ How to Create Local Change

✓ **Join a Mutual Aid Network** – Help neighbors with food, housing, and resources.

✓ **Organize Local Skill-Sharing Events** – Teach and learn skills that promote self-sufficiency.

✓ **Start Community Initiatives** – Create local co-ops, farmers' markets, or trade networks.

✓ **Encourage Civic Engagement** – Educate and mobilize your community on key issues.

☐ **Action Step: Find one local initiative you can support or start your own community project.**

Step 6: Use Technology for Empowerment, Not Control

☐ *Technology can be a tool for freedom or oppression—use it strategically.*

☐ Digital Resistance & Empowerment

☐ **Use Encrypted Messaging** – Protect your privacy with apps like Signal.

☐ **Support Decentralized Platforms** – Move away from corporate-controlled social media.

☐ **Educate Yourself on Cybersecurity** – Learn about VPNs, encryption, and online anonymity.

☐ **Use Social Media for Activism** – Share independent news, organize movements, and educate others.

☐ **Action Step: Secure your digital life by switching to at least one privacy-focused tool.**

Step 7: Develop Independent Skills & Self-Sufficiency

☐ *The less you rely on the system, the harder it is for the system to control you.*

☐ Essential Skills for an Independent Future

✓ **Grow Your Own Food** – Even a small garden increases independence.

✓ **Learn Basic Survival Skills** – Know how to purify water, fix things, and prepare for crises.
✓ **Gain Financial Literacy** – Understand investing, saving, and wealth-building outside traditional banks.
✓ **Develop a High-Income Skill** – Coding, writing, digital marketing, or entrepreneurship can create financial freedom.

▢ **Action Step: Choose one new skill to start learning this month.**

Step 8: Stay Consistent & Keep Taking Action

▢ *Change doesn't happen in a day—it happens because of consistent, small efforts over time.*

▢ **How to Stay Committed to Your Mission**

▢ **Set Small, Achievable Goals** – Progress is built one step at a time.
▢ **Surround Yourself with Like-Minded People** – Join communities that keep you inspired and motivated.
▢ **Avoid Burnout** – Take breaks, but never disengage completely.
▢ **Teach & Inspire Others** – The more people you educate, the more powerful the movement becomes.

▢ **Action Step: Make a 3-month plan for what actions you will take and track your progress.**

Final Thought: You Have the Power to Change the World

▢ **The system thrives when people do nothing—but collapses when enough people take action.**
▢ **You don't need to be famous, rich, or powerful—every great movement began with ordinary people making small, bold choices.**
▢ **The future is not something you wait for—it's something you build, step by step.**

The roadmap is in your hands. The only question left is: Will you start today? ▢

CONCLUSION: YOU ARE MORE POWERFUL THAN YOU THINK

"The people who are crazy enough to think they can change the world are the ones who do." — Steve Jobs

Y ou have reached the end of this book, but this is not the end of your journey—it is just the beginning.

If you take away one lesson from these pages, let it be this:

☐ **The world does not change because of politicians, corporations, or the wealthy elite. The world changes because of ordinary citizens—people like you—who decide that enough is enough.**

The Power Has Always Been Yours

☐ **History proves it.** Every revolution, movement, and major social change started with **one person or a small group who refused to stay silent.**

☐ **Corporations and governments fear it.** That's why they

239

spend billions **manipulating, distracting, and dividing people —because they know that when enough citizens unite, their power crumbles.**

◻ **Your choices shape the future.** Every dollar you spend, every vote you cast, every conversation you have—**these are acts of power.**

The only thing standing between you and making a difference **is the belief that you can't.**

What Happens Next is Up to You

You now have a roadmap, tools, and real-world examples of how ordinary people have transformed their communities, economies, and governments.

The question is: **What will you do with this knowledge?**

You can choose to:

✓ **Take action today.** Start small, but start now—boycott an unethical company, attend a community meeting, or learn a new skill.

✓ **Educate and inspire others.** Share what you've learned, have conversations, and help others see their power.

✓ **Stay committed.** Change is not a one-time event—it's a lifelong journey.

Or you can **do nothing.**

You can close this book, return to life as usual, and allow the system to continue unchecked. You can let others decide your future.

But deep down, you know the truth:

◻ **The world will not fix itself. The people who take action today will shape tomorrow.** ◻

Final Words: The Future is Waiting—What Will You Do?

If history has taught us anything, it is this:

☐ **The system survives when people do nothing.**

☐ **But when enough people take action, the system must change.**

This is not just an idea—it is a fact, proven time and time again.

So, will you watch history unfold from the sidelines?
Or will you be one of the people who shapes it?

The choice is yours. The power is yours. The future is yours.

Now go and change the world. ☐

EPILOGUE

"A single person cannot change the world, but they can start a movement that will."

You have now seen the truth that has been hidden in plain sight:

☐ **Ordinary people have always shaped history.**
☐ **The system relies on your compliance to maintain its power.**
☐ **Your choices—no matter how small—create ripples of change.**

This is not theory. **This is reality.**

The next chapter of history is unwritten. It will be shaped by those who refuse to remain silent, who take action despite fear, and who recognize that **power was never meant to be hoarded by the few—it belongs to the many.**

The Journey Doesn't End Here

This book was never meant to be just words on a page. **It is a call to action, a blueprint, a spark.**

But a spark alone is not enough. It must be followed by action.

☐ **What will you do today to reclaim your power?**

What change will you create in your community?
How will you challenge the system that thrives on your inaction?

This journey is not easy. It will be frustrating. It will test your patience. There will be moments where change feels slow, where the system seems too big, too strong.

But remember this:

The greatest revolutions in history began with a single act of defiance.

The world needs more people who refuse to say **"That's just the way things are."**
The world needs more people who will say **"No, I will not accept this."**

The world needs you.

Final Thought: The Future is Watching

One day, someone will look back at this moment in history.
They will study the choices people made, the actions they took, and the courage they showed.

What will they see?

A generation that stood by and let corruption, greed, and injustice continue?
Or a generation that **stood up, spoke out, and took action**—one person at a time?

The future is watching. History is waiting. The revolution begins with you.

Go. Take action. Be the change.

AFTERWORD

"The most powerful weapon on earth is the human soul on fire." — Ferdinand Foch

You've made it to the end of this book, but the real work is just beginning.

If there is one thing I hope you take away, it's this: **you were never powerless.**

The system—whether political, economic, or social—wants you to believe that change is impossible, that your actions don't matter, that the world is controlled by forces too big for any individual to influence.

But that is a lie.

History belongs to those who refuse to accept things as they are. The ones who act, who speak, who organize, who resist, who build.

And now, **it's your turn.**

What Comes Next?

This book may have ended, but your journey is just beginning. **What will you do with what you've learned?**

Here are three simple steps to keep moving forward:

 Take action today. Even the smallest step—a conversation, a boycott, a vote—starts a ripple effect.

 Educate others. Share these ideas, inspire your community, and encourage others to reclaim their power.

 Stay committed. Change is not instant. It takes persistence, resilience, and a refusal to back down.

You don't need to change the entire world in one day. But you do need to start.

Final Words: The Future is Unwritten

The most dangerous thing you can believe is that **your actions don't matter.**

 Every great movement began with ordinary people doing extraordinary things.

 Every system that seemed unbreakable was dismantled by those who refused to obey.

 Every revolution started because someone, somewhere, decided that enough was enough.

You have **more power than you think.** The question is: **What will you do with it?**

The world is waiting. Now go make history.

ACKNOWLEDGEMENT

No book is written in isolation, and The Power of the Ordinary Citizen is no exception. This work is the result of countless conversations, inspirations, and lessons learned from those who have dedicated their lives to challenging the status quo.

To the Activists, Dreamers, and Fighters

To the countless individuals—past and present—who have fought for justice, equality, and freedom, often at great personal cost: **this book exists because of you.** Your courage, persistence, and refusal to accept oppression have shaped history and continue to inspire those who dare to dream of a better world.

To the Readers Who Refuse to Be Silent

This book is for you—the people who **question, resist, and take action.** Every reader who picks up this book and chooses to act, even in the smallest way, is proof that ordinary people hold extraordinary power. Thank you for believing that change is possible and for being part of the movement to make it happen.

To My Family and Friends

Your unwavering support, patience, and encouragement have made this journey possible. Thank you for the late-night discussions, the debates, and the endless inspiration that shaped my thinking and, ultimately, this book.

To Those Who Challenge the System

To the journalists, whistleblowers, educators, and truth-seekers who risk everything to expose corruption and empower others —**your work is invaluable.** Your dedication to truth and justice is a reminder that knowledge is one of the most powerful tools in the fight for change.

To the Future Changemakers

To those who will read this book and **use it as a catalyst for action**—thank you. The world needs more people who refuse to accept "the way things are" and instead ask, **"How can things be better?"**

This book is dedicated to you all. **Together, we are unstoppable.**

ABOUT THE AUTHOR

Abdellatif Raji

Abdellatif Raji is a writer, thinker, and advocate for social change, political empowerment, and economic justice. Passionate about the power of the ordinary citizen, he believes that history is not shaped by the elite but by those who dare to challenge the status quo.

Through his work, Raji explores how individuals can reclaim their power in a world increasingly dominated by corporations, governments, and media influence. His writing combines historical insights, real-world examples, and practical strategies to equip readers with the tools to take meaningful action.

With a background in political science, activism, journalism, education, Raji has spent years studying grassroots movements, economic systems, and political resistance. His work is dedicated to those who refuse to stay silent, who seek to disrupt oppressive systems, and who believe that a better world is possible—if enough people take action.

Connect with the Author

Website: https://www.abdellatifraji.com/
Email: author@abdellatifraji.com

For speaking engagements, collaborations, or to join the movement, reach out via contact@abdellatifraji.com.

The revolution begins with you. Stay informed, stay engaged, and take action.

BOOKS BY THIS AUTHOR

Heaven Is Under The Feet Of Governments

Heaven Is Under the Feet of Governments is not just a book —it's a clarion call for a new kind of leadership, one that dares to align governance with the deepest ethical and spiritual values of humanity. Written by visionary thinker Abdellatif Raji, this groundbreaking work introduces the Maqasid model— a transformative governance framework that goes beyond the mechanics of administration and enters the realm of moral purpose.

Imagine a world where policy doesn't merely chase economic metrics, but seeks justice, compassion, and collective well-being. Raji argues that such a world is not only possible— it's urgently necessary. The Maqasid model, while rooted in Islamic jurisprudence, transcends religious boundaries, offering universal principles that can reshape governance in any cultural context. It prioritizes the protection of life, intellect, dignity, community, and the environment—objectives that resonate across faiths and philosophies.

This book doesn't stop at theory. It delivers a concrete action plan for integrating ethical values into policy, building inclusive societies, and addressing modern challenges like inequality and environmental degradation. With clarity and conviction, Raji dispels the misconception that spirituality in governance implies theocracy. Instead, he presents a compelling case for ethics-driven governance that respects diversity and pluralism.

Whether you're a policymaker, academic, social leader, or concerned global citizen, Heaven Is Under the Feet of Governments offers an inspiring roadmap for building a world where prosperity is guided by purpose. Dive in—and discover how governance, when grounded in conscience, can truly uplift humanity.

Reimagine leadership. Redefine progress. Read this book—and join the movement for ethical transformation.

The Human Journey

The Human Journey by Abdellatif Raji is more than a book—it's a profound invitation to reorient your life around purpose, clarity, and eternal significance. Imagine a map that not only charts the origins of existence and the destiny of the soul, but also illuminates each moment of your life with meaning. This is that map. This is your guide.

Raji doesn't merely explore theology—he redefines what it means to be human. Grounded in Islamic tradition yet enriched with universal philosophical insight, The Human Journey constructs a compelling framework that weaves together faith, reason, and spiritual awareness. It begins where all understanding must: with the knowledge of God. Not as an abstract ideal, but as the Essential Reality, the source of all existence and meaning.

From there, Raji confronts the modern crises of nihilism and materialism, offering a transformative vision of life as intentional, divinely orchestrated, and ethically charged. Human beings, he asserts, are not aimless creatures but entrusted vicegerents—moral agents with a sacred role in creation. Every breath we take, every decision we make, is part of an ultimate test leading to Paradise or Hell.

But this journey is not a solitary endeavor. Raji skillfully unpacks the core structure of faith: Islam (practice), Īmān (belief), and Iḥsān (spiritual excellence). He leads you through this tripartite path, showing how ritual, belief, and inner consciousness converge to shape a holistic life of devotion and dignity.

Culminating in a powerful exposition of the Maqāṣid al-Sharīʿah —the higher ethical objectives of divine law—Raji presents a blueprint for societal well-being grounded in justice, intellect, family, community, and faith. This is not religious dogma; it is an ethical roadmap for human flourishing.

The Human Journey is a must-read for seekers of truth, students of theology, and anyone yearning for meaning in an increasingly chaotic world. It challenges you to think deeply, live intentionally, and walk your path with purpose.

Read this book—and awaken to the journey you were always meant to live.

www.ingramcontent.com/pod-product-compliance
Lightning Source LLC
Chambersburg PA
CBHW071017280326
41935CB00011B/1382